Elizabeth Ingrid Hauser

Princess Crafts

Illustrated by
Lisa Parett

Sterling Publishing Co., Inc.
New York

This book is dedicated with oodles of love and endless thanks to my mother.
Mom, you will always be the fairest one of all in my magic mirror. —Elizabeth

Edited by Jeanette Green
Photographs by Michael Hnatov

Library of Congress Cataloging-in-Publication Data

Hauser, Elizabeth.
    Princess crafts / Elizabeth Ingrid Hauser.
        p. cm.
    Summary: Provides illustrations and step-by-step instructions for sewing, decorating, and creating princess costumes, decorations, games, and refreshments. Each project is rated by degree of difficulty.
    Includes index.
    ISBN 0-8069-7116-9
    1. Handicraft—Juvenile literature. 2. Children—Clothing—Juvenile literature.
    3. Princesses in art—Juvenile literature. [1.Handicraft. 2. Costume. 3. Princesses.] I. Title.
    TT171.H485 2003
    745.5--dc   212003000289

1   3   5   7   9   10   8   6   4   2

Published by Sterling Publishing Co., Inc.
387 Park Avenue South, New York, N.Y. 10016
© 2003 by Elizabeth Ingrid Hauser
Distributed in Canada by Sterling Publishing
C/o Canadian Manda Group, One Atlantic Avenue, Suite 105
Toronto, Ontario, Canada M6K 3E7
Distributed in Great Britain and Europe by Chris Lloyd at Orca Book Services,
Stanley House, Fleets Lane, Poole BH15 3AJ, England
Distributed in Australia by Capricorn Link (Australia) Pty. Ltd.
P.O. Box 704, Windsor, NSW 2756 Australia
Printed in China
All rights reserved

Sterling ISBN 0-8069-7116-9

Our Model Princesses: Amanda Horowitz, Angela Goscilo, Annabelle, Carolyn Goscilo, Emmanuelle
"Chi-Chi" Egodigwe, Emily Kirk, Genesis Zelaya, Isabelle, Krista Bannon, Lauren Nnenna Egodigwe,
Natalie Morales, Rebekah Lynn Ortiz, and Sitina Xu. And Model Princes: Sam Horowitz and Brendan Doyle.

Acknowledgments

Many thanks to Folkmanis® Puppets for their green dragon and the Manhattan store The Enchanted Forest for lending it; the dragon appears on p. 13. Our other plush "models" are courtesy of Manhattan Toy Company. The lovely poodle Gigi wears the Court Jester Canine Cap. Griffin Goat, Betty Bunny, Bernice Bear, Rhoda the Rompalot (horse), and the mice and birdie from the Newbies collection model the dwarf caps in "Dwarfs Aplenty" (pp. 16 and 30).

We're grateful to Lynette Santiago, Tabitha Rivera, Rafael Morales, Pamela Horn, Marilyn Kretzer, Margaret La Salle, and Maryanne Bannon for suggesting models; Nancy Baker for our Ontario model; Claire Bazinet, Laura Saunders-Egodigwe, and Shirley Saunders for the many cozy slumber party props. Many helpful parents of our models made this book possible. Also many thanks to Jeannine C. Ford and Michael Hnatov, and Louis Díaz at Michael Hnatov Photography for many favors.

Contents

The Secret to Being a
True Princess

Once upon a time, there lived a lovely young girl with a smile as sweet as gumdrops and a heart to match. Her name was...Oh, you're reading this book? I thought you already were a princess! Well, whatever the case, even a true princess needs some pointers now and again.

What makes a true princess, you ask? Years of research on the topic have led me to develop this formula:

Kindness + Loyalty + Spirit
x Inner Beauty = True Princess

If you apply this formula to your life, you will become an ever-most-shining true princess in no time!

Materials Fit for Royalty

It's always wise to keep a treasure chest full of crafty goodies. Here are some precious materials I like to keep around my palace.

Endless Array of Glitter
Sequins, Beads, and Buttons
Fabric Flowers, Leaves, and Butterflies
Felt Rectangles
Colorful Fabric
Rickrack
Ribbon of All Kinds
Lace and Eyelet Trim
Marabou Trim
Tinsel
Glittery Sticker Paper
Pipe Cleaners
All Sorts of Styrofoam Shapes

Junk with Potential
Old Clothes and Jewelry
Variety of Paintbrushes
Really Good Craft Glue (I use Aleene's Tacky Glue.)
Regular Old School Glue (great for glitterizing)
Faux Gems (Faux is a really fancy way of saying "fake.")
Pom-Poms (You can even find these in a sparkly or beadable version.)
Gifts from Nature (I've been collecting pine cones, sticks, and pretty rocks for years.)

Array of Scissors (one for fabric, one for paper, ones with special edges, etc.)
Acrylic Craft Paint (I recommend the pearlescent; it's so rich and shimmery.)

Be a Thrifty Princess!

Just because you look as though you're wearing the Crown jewels doesn't mean you paid a fortune. A thrifty princess always knows when and where to shop and how to winkle out good deals. Here are some helpful hints.

✳ Shop after big holidays! Some of the best tinsel, ribbon, and other craft supplies get marked way down.

✳ Scope out places like garage or tag sales, thrift and surplus shops, and 99¢ stores.

✳ Leave no stone unturned. A trip to the basement or a walk in the woods may unearth a wealth of crafty treasures.

✳ Save scraps! Eventually, they'll come in handy.

✳ Trade supplies with a friend. One person's garbage is another's gold mine.

✳ Remember, you can't buy style, and you've got plenty of that. If something super inexpensive strikes your fancy, but you don't know what to do with it, just pick it up and wait. A splendid new craft may be just around the corner.

The Fine Art of Improvisation

It's important to understand that you may not always be able to find exactly what's on the Royal requests list. That's where your crafty noodle comes into play. Don't have any faux gems? Use sequins. No beads? Use buttons. The same is true for attaching one object to another (or "adhering"). If that outrageously gorgeous fabric flower is just too heavy for craft glue, use clear packing tape or ask for permission to use a hot glue gun. It's perfectly OK to dream up all sorts of inventive substitutions. In fact, life is all about problem-solving, so be proud of this skill.

Also, don't be afraid of making mistakes; they happen...even if you're a princess. Ghastly gobs of glue or unsightly stitches can almost always be hidden by adding more glitter, sequins, or some other sparkling embellishment. What's important is that you experiment with different artful techniques until you find your own personal princess style.

Know Thy Glitter

Any princess worth her tiara should know how to apply glitter ("glitterize"). To properly do so, first know thy glitter. Here's a crash course.

Finishes...

Metallic Pure reflection...This is wonderful for imitating silver and gold.

Iridescent Rainbowlike shimmer...Fairy princesses love this stuff.

Holographic Prismatic in its reflective qualities.

Glow-in-the-Dark I think you know what this one does.

Shapes...

Round The look is very even and pristine.

Square This has a little more of a rugged effect.

Specialty (such as hearts, stars, and moons) These are a jackpot of glitter.

Grain Sizes...

Ultra-Fine This glitter is almost like pixie dust and is used in lip gloss. It's also great for outlining shapes.

Fine The perfect multi-purpose glitter

Medium Appears more twinkly...like little gems

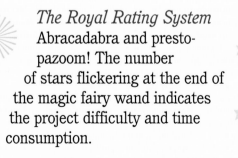

The Royal Rating System
Abracadabra and presto-pazoom! The number of stars flickering at the end of the magic fairy wand indicates the project difficulty and time consumption.

Zing, a royal snap!

Requires moderate wand use.

Hold onto your tiara. This one will take a little more hocus-pocusing!

The Time-Honored Tradition of Glitterization

For centuries, this noble craft has been handed down from one royal family to the next! The path to artful "glitterization" (we made up this word), however, is not all sparkles and sunshine. As with most things in life, a wee bit of practice will be needed in order for you to become a pro. The basic formula is pretty simple:

Glitter sprinkled over glue = Super-sparkly glitterization.

Once you've mastered the genius of glitterization, you'll look like a fashion fairy tale come true in no time! Here are some tips.

* *The best type of glue for glitterizing is a thin one, like plain old school glue.*
* *When coating your object with glue, try to make sure the glue is evenly distributed.*
* *Apply glitter only in the places you want highlighted. It never pays to accentuate features that aren't that extraordinary (unless you're covering up a mistake...).*
* *If glitterizing a large object, always sprinkle glitter over a clean sheet of paper or a box, and then save the excess.*
* *You can even try mixing glitters to create your own!*
* *If glitterizing a small object, fill a clean, empty butter tub with glitter, place your glue-coated object inside, seal the lid, and shake. When you take your object out, it will sparkle like magic. You can reuse the glitter tub for other projects.*
* *Painting your object with a layer of color before you glitterize (especially with an iridescent glitter) creates an ethereal glow.*
* *Although this princess prefers to glitterize the old-fashioned way, some glitter glues and glitter pens are great for writing and come in a variety of colors.*

How to Use Your Templates

Using the templates in this book is easy. Trace or photocopy the pattern you wish to use. If it isn't the size you want, reduce or enlarge it. Then cut your pattern out and lay it on the flip side of the material you are using for your project (sticker paper, fabric, felt, etc). Follow the outline with a pen or marker. When you lift up your template, your shape will be completely drawn. Cut it out and voilà...you're all set. You'll find the templates on pages 92 to 95.

The Art of Tacking

Some princess projects call for tacking, which is not so difficult once you get the hang of it. First thread your needle. Then position the two pieces of fabric you wish to tack. Make a couple of tiny loops, joining both pieces together. Now tie both ends of your thread together and trim the excess. Don't let anyone tell you that this is a tacky way of doing things!

Classic Princess

When you're a classic, you set the standard. You shy away from fads and go for timeless chic. You become legendary.

The same holds true for the Classic Princess. Her sublime grace and courtly elegance are what others look up to. She's what fairy tales are made of.

Classic Princess Skirt

There are some essentials a princess just cannot live without...

Her Royal Majesty Requests

- Floor-Length Skirt
  (flowing if possible)
- Oodles of Netting or Tulle
- Lace, Ruffle, or Ribbon Trim
- Marabou Trim
- Fabric Flowers or Butterflies
- Faux Gems, Sequins, or
  Beads
- Glitter
- Scissors
- Needle and Thread
- Craft Glue

Cut the netting into long, flowing, petallike shapes or a simple overskirt shape. Using your needle and thread, tack these pretty petals to the waist of your skirt. Then tack your marabou trim to the netting's edge or so that it flows alongside the petals. Now decorate by gluing glitter, gems, sequins, beads, butterflies, flowers, and other trim wherever you feel fit. Allow at least an hour for drying time, and remember...don't skirt any details!

Classic Princess Bodice

This one's a piece of princess cake. First lay out your bodice top and decide where you want all of your decorative frou-frous and frillies to be. Then glue them in place. Wait at least an hour for everything to dry. Wear with poise.

Her Royal Majesty Requests

- Bodice-Type Top
  (Even a tank top will do.)
- Marabou, Lace, Ruffle,
  or Ribbon Trim
- Faux Gems, Sequins, or Beads
- Fabric Flowers and Butterflies
- Glitter
- Scissors
- Craft Glue

Captivating Cameo Necklace

The cameo is a piece of jewelry that says, "I accessorize with only the finest." To make this nifty necklace, first cut a tiny piece of felt into a fancy frame or oval shape. Line the edges with glue and add glitter. If desired, make an even smaller fancy frame or oval, glitterize and glue that to the center of your larger one. Then glue an especially pretty bead (one that you want to show off...like a butterfly or a heart) to the middle of your frame and ta-da!—You have a captivating cameo. Now glue your cameo to the middle of a colorful ribbon and tie it around your neck. Ah! Such style and grace!

Classic Princess Hat

Cut your sticker paper into stripes, hearts, stars, or any other shape you feel fit to adorn your hat. Adhere your fancy shapes where desired. Then cut an extra long piece of netting and fold it in half. Stick the folded end of the netting into the tip of the cone. (You may need to cut a slightly wider opening.) Place on your head and take an elegant stroll around your courtyard.

Her Royal Majesty Requests

- Solid-Colored Party Hat
- Glittery Sticker Paper
- Netting
- Scissors
- Craft Glue

The Perfect Princess Pocketbook

1. Fold your felt in half width-wise. Then glue the two outer edges together forming a pocketbook.

2. Cut beaded or ribbon trim a little longer than the length you would like for your handle. Glue one end of the trim just inside the edge of your pocketbook. Now repeat with the other end and edge.

3. Add lace trim across the top and glue a pom-pom in the middle. Embellish the rest with fabric butterflies, faux gems, glitter, or anything else that strikes your fancy.

Her Royal Majesty Requests

- Felt Rectangle
- Beaded or Ribbon Trim
- Lace Trim
- Sparkle Pom-Pom
- Faux Gems
- Glitter
- Craft Scissors
- Craft Glue
- Fabric Butterflies or Flowers

Princess Glamour Gloves

Delicate hands require delicate care, and what better way to protect them than with gorgeous gloves. A royal bonus is how elegant you'll look carrying your matching pocketbook! Measure and cut your marabou so that you have two pieces that perfectly fit around each glove. Trim one of your gloves with marabou by tacking it in place every inch or so. Repeat with the other piece of marabou. Finally, glue sequins, glitter, or both onto the top part of your glove for adornment. Now step out onto the balcony and wave to your people.

Her Royal Majesty Requests

- Pair of Party Gloves
- Marabou Trim
- Sequins or Glitter
- Scissors
- Needle and Thread
- Craft Glue

11

Razzling-Dazzling Tiara

A true princess requires a tiara, and you, my dear, are no exception.

Her Royal Majesty Requests

- Plain or Glitterized Headband (*I found mine in a pretty zigzag shape.*)
- 2 Pipe Cleaners
- Glitter
- Faux Gems, Beads, or Sequins
- Wire Clippers or Pliers
- Craft Glue

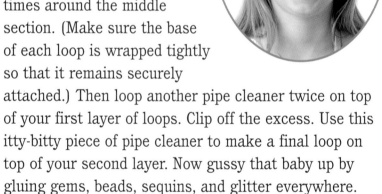

If your headband is not already glitterized, now is the time to do so. Turning your headband sideways, loop a pipe cleaner evenly 3 times around the middle section. (Make sure the base of each loop is wrapped tightly so that it remains securely attached.) Then loop another pipe cleaner twice on top of your first layer of loops. Clip off the excess. Use this itty-bitty piece of pipe cleaner to make a final loop on top of your second layer. Now gussy that baby up by gluing gems, beads, sequins, and glitter everywhere. Allow drying time and place delicately atop your head. If the tiara fits, wear it! (Don't worry; it will fit.)

Brother's Fire-Breathing Dragon Hat

Does your brother hoard all his toys and chase you around the castle like he owns it? Well, now it's time to put him in his proper place by turning him into the mean ole dragon he is.

Her Royal Majesty Requests

- Baseball Cap
- 2 Medium Styrofoam Balls
- 2 Small Styrofoam Balls
- Assorted Felt Rectangles
- Assorted Feathers
- Glittery Paper (optional)
- Large Googly Eyes
- Glitter
- Patterned Fabric (optional)
- Sponge Brush
- Butter Tub with Lid
- Scissors
- Craft Glue and Plain Old School Glue

1. Dash a generous amount of glitter into your tub. Using a sponge brush, coat one Styrofoam ball with glue. Place that sticky, gluey ball into the glitter tub, seal the lid, and shake for 15 seconds. Then stop, unseal the lid, and take out the glittery ball. Repeat the same steps with the other ball. Then add a googly eye to the middle of each medium-size ball so that they look like dragon peepers. If you wish to add eyelashes out of felt or glittery paper, do so at this time. Glue the dragon eyes onto the brim of your brother's hat, leaving a tiny bit of room behind them. Then glue the 2 smaller glittery balls in front for nostrils.

2. Get all fired up...because the next part is blazing good fun. Cut teeth, scales, tufts, and flames out of felt. Glue them onto your dragon along with just the right touch of glitter and feathers. For extra fun, add patterned fabric and glittery paper. The more you embellish, the more you will be able to laugh at your brother when he wears this special hat. Well, the little monster should enjoy it, too.

✳ *If you do not have a brother, borrow the boy next door.*

13

Your Carriage Awaits

Why design a princess bicycle when you can simply go out to buy one? The answer is clear: those bikes are just for wannabe princesses. A true blueblood always travels in custom-designed style.

After you've unearthed a treasure trove of materials, get your creative gears in motion with some of the decorative options. Then ride off into the sunset.

Her Royal Majesty Requests

- Old Bicycle
- Sparkly Sticker Paper or Tape
- Curling Ribbon
- Marabou Trim
- Plastic Garland
- Tinsel
- Package Bows and Frou-Frous
- Plastic or Fabric Flowers and Butterflies
- Glitter
- Jingle Bells
- Pom-Poms (Beadable ones are great for this project as well.)
- Bicycle Mirror, Horn, Basket
- Safety Flag
- Scissors
- Clear Heavy-Duty Packing Tape
- Craft Glue

WARNING: Make sure that nothing can get caught in the gears of your bike. A tumbling, bumbling princess is not a pretty sight.

❀ Decorate your spokes, handlebars, frame, or bike seat with sparkly sticker paper.

❀ Add a bicycle mirror, basket, and horn for super embellishment.

❀ Trim your basket with marabou and garland.

❀ Weave curling ribbon in between the spokes.

❀ Add bows and frou-frous everywhere so that your bike looks like a festival on wheels.

❀ Stick tinsel, garland, and curling ribbon to your bicycle with clear packing tape.

❀ Use tape to get flowers and butterflies to stay in place.

❀ Make your safety flag into a princess banner.

❀ Add jingle bells to your handlebars or seat with ribbon.

❀ Add pom-poms everywhere.

❀ Glitterize everything you deem appropriate.

Court Jester Canine Cap

If your dog keeps you howling with laughter, then this project is for you!

Decide which type of canine you will be using (a real one or the plush kind). Copy the Court Jester Canine Cap template as is or enlarge it on a photocopier so that it looks like it is about 2 to 3 inches wider than your doggy's head. Cut out the template and trace around it on the fabric you have selected. After you're done, trace another one. Now cut out these 2 pieces and lay one of them flat on a clean surface with the fun pattern facing down.

Carefully, start to glue along the perimeter, keeping the bottom edge glue-free. When you have glued about 3 inches, stop and lay the other Court Jester Canine Cap piece directly on top of the one being glued. Make sure that the edges line up and that the fabric's pattern is facing you. Continue until your entire cap is glued (minus the bottom, of course). Allow about an hour for drying time and then tack on your jingle bells (or pom-poms) using a needle and thread. OK! Perch that jingle hat on your pooch's head! The two of you can now tell jokes back 'n' forth, laughing yourselves silly.

* If you feel that your Court Jester Canine Cap needs to be more secure, attach 2 long ribbons to it so that you can tie a cute little bow just beneath doggy's chin.

* Cap a little too floppy? Fill it with some stuffing or even cotton balls.

Her Royal Majesty Requests

- *Fun Patterned Fabric (like dots)*
- *2 Small Jingle Bells or Pom-poms*
- *Needle and Thread*
- *Marker*
- *Pencil and Paper*
- *Scissors*
- *Glue*

Jokes to Share With Your Dog

Q: What do you call a dog who's always in a bad mood?

A: A wet Poodle.

Q: Why did the Dalmatian cross the road?

A: Because she spotted something on the other side.

Q: What happens when a Yorky eats too much ham?

A: He turns into a Porkshire Terrier.

Ha! Ha! Ha! With jokes this funny you might want to see if the local canine comedy clubs are hiring.

Dragon's Breath Candy Mix

Only for the bravest of princesses.

Royal Highbrow Ingredients

- *1 cup Red Hots or Cinnamon Candy*
- *½ cup Sour Cherry Candy*
- *¼ cup Lemon Drops*

Find a bowl that looks worthy of the tantalizing candy it is about to hold. Pour all your ingredients together and mix. Nibble a piece or two to see if you can handle the heat. Increase candy intake as your tongue becomes accustomed to the burning-hot flames.

The Frog Prince

Ribbit-ribbit. Frogs are kind of cute, but come on now, would you really want to kiss one? Well, that's exactly how the princess feels in the original story of "The Frog Prince." In fact, she finds him so slimy and repulsive that she throws him against her bedroom wall and breaks the spell with a clunk on the head rather than a kiss on the lips.

Luckily, over time the tale was softened. Our Royal Froggyness isn't the only one who is fortunate; we princesses are, too. Kissing is so much more fun than walloping. (Look this word up, if you don't already know it...A princess should always be improving her vocabulary.) So get ready for some amphibious affection.

Golden Ball Jewelry

The princess's favorite plaything in all the world was a golden ball. Now really, is that very sensible? Gold is extremely heavy and when she dropped it into the well, it kerplunked straight to the bottom. Thank goodness that, although cold-blooded, the Frog Prince had a warm little heart and rescued her golden ball from the murky depths.

You can recreate all that shimmery splendor by buying gold garland or ribbon and instead of decorating a tree or package, decorate yourself! Clear packing tape is dandy for holding your luminous creations together.

ALERT! If anyone tries to hand you that old line about "all that shimmers isn't gold," tell them that they're simply "full of fool's gold." Ha! This princess often enjoys getting the last laugh (even if it's only in her imagination).

Frog Prince Beanbag Pal ✦ ✦

Before you start any kissing, you first need to find a frog. And what better way to find the perfect frog than to design one yourself?

1. Transfer the frog pattern onto both pieces of fabric and cut them out.

2. Lay one frog down so that the print faces the table. Take your glue (make sure the tip is nice and unclogged), and starting at his tush (derriere or bottom), follow the outline of your frog partway with glue.

3. Stop and then carefully, carefully, carefully place the other frog shape directly on top of the one with glue (print facing you) so that everything matches up. Delicately press the edges. Repeat the gluing and pressing process until you reach about an inch before where you began. Wait at least an hour for the glue to dry.

4. In the opening (the inch left unglued), fill the little guy up with barley (you may want to use a funnel made out of paper). Glue the rest of him shut, clamp secure with the clothespin, and allow adequate drying time.

5. Now make a little frog-size crown out of felt and glitterize. Finally, give that guy a personality by adding hearts for eyes and nice big lips. Oh my! He's so kissable!

Her Royal Majesty Requests

- *Two 8×10-inch Rectangles of Fabric*
- *2 Heart-Shaped Buttons, Pieces of Felt, or Gems*
- *Lip-Shaped Button or Piece of Felt*
- *Small Piece of Felt (for his crown)*
- *Glitter*
- *Uncooked Pearl Barley*
- *Colored Marker (like the color of your fabric)*
- *Fabric Scissors*
- *Clothespin*
- *Glue*

*H*I*N*T*

To keep the fabric from fraying, mix a little bit of glue with a little bit of water and paint your frog's edges with it.

Frog Prints Stationery

Alas, with the advent of e-mail, letter writing is quickly becoming a lost art form. This has brought a tear to the eye of many a fine young frog since amphibians don't receive e-mail. So go ahead. Brush up on your penmanship and make a frog happy.

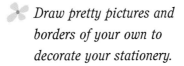
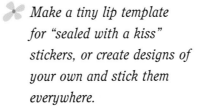

Stationery comes in all shapes and sizes, so don't feel bogged down in any way. Try some of these techniques, and then create your own.

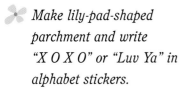

- Make lily-pad-shaped parchment and write "X O X O" or "Luv Ya" in alphabet stickers.

- Doll up a cute paper frog princess with gems, sequins, and shaped confetti, and stick her somewhere special.

- Cut origami or decorative paper into hearts or lips—just the perfect shape for you to write sweet little messages to your flippered little love.

- Draw pretty pictures and borders of your own to decorate your stationery.

- Make a tiny lip template for "sealed with a kiss" stickers, or create designs of your own and stick them everywhere.

- Design an elegant scroll shape out of decorative paper and pretend you live in the Old World.

Her Royal Majesty Requests

- Brightly Colored Paper
- Brightly Colored Envelopes
- Brightly Colored Origami or Decorative Paper
- Faux Gems, Sequins, and Shaped Confetti (I found tiny lips.)
- Shimmery Sticker Paper
- Tiny Alphabet Stickers
- Colored Markers
- Scissors
- Plain Old Regular School Glue

Take pride in your work, and be happy knowing that these personalized touches will undoubtedly knock him off his lily pad.

Frilly Feathered Quill

Words of love will fly from your heart to your fingertips with this fancy pen.

First glue the gigantic plume to the cap of your pen. Let it dry a wee bit and then lay your pen cap in the middle of your ribbon and wrap both ends down around the base of your plume to secure it even more. Tie the ends of your ribbon into a knot and snip off the excess. You may want to add a dab of glue to the knot so that it doesn't come undone. Decorate with sequins or faux gems. Write a verse or two that will woo him off his little webbed feet.

Her Royal Majesty Requests

- *Capped Pen with Pink or Green Ink*
- *Gigantic Plume (This means a really big feather.)*
- *1 Foot of Thin Ribbon*
- *2 or 3 Sequins or Faux Gems*
- *Scissors*
- *Craft Glue*

Magical, Lovely Words for Wooing

Good looks and charm aren't the only way to win the tiny green heart of your true love. A magical sweet something written in a love note or whispered gently into the wind (or even his ear, if you're brave enough) may also do wonders.

"Gumdrops, Cookies, Muffins, and Pie.
  I Love You as Much as the Stars in the Sky!"

"Roses are Red,
  Violets are Blue,
  You're Slimy and Green,
  But I Still Love You!"

"Hocus-Pocus Cutesy-Poo-Locus
  You Make My Eyes See Outta Focus!"

"Splish-Splash, Kerplunk-Kerplunk.
  You're Sweeter than a Chocolate Chunk!"

"Whiz, Bang, Smackeroo!
  I Love You.
  I Do, I Do."

Now it's your turn to pen a line or two.

Warning: Some wannabe princes think that magical, lovely words are nothing but "icky girl stuff." Never mind them. They are not even at frog level...they are toads. Be yourself, and say how you truly feel. A real prince will appreciate your honesty.

Pucker-Up Princess... Kissing Gloss

Guaranteed to transform that very special frog into a handsome prince...

- 2 Tablespoons Petroleum Jelly
- 1 Teaspoon Honey
- 2 Drops Flavored Extract (peppermint, vanilla, or almond work beautifully)
- Sprinkle of Ultra-Fine Iridescent Glitter (Make sure it says "nontoxic.")
- Mom's Leftover, Cleaned-Out Make-up Jars
- Sliver of Color (from one of Mom's old tubes of lipstick—optional) (Be sure to ask first.)
- Cotton Swab

Mix your ingredients in a small jar. Stir until well blended with a cotton swab. Apply gloss to your lips with the swab, and kiss the most desirable frog in sight.

✴ Jazz up make-up jars with sticker paper, fabric flowers, and faux gems.

Smoochy-Woochy Kissing-Gloss Tote

Her Royal Majesty Requests

- *Pink Felt*
- *Ribbon*
- *Faux Gems (optional)*
- *Pink Glitter*
- *Dark Pink Marker*
- *Craft Scissors*
- *Glue*

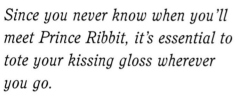

Since you never know when you'll meet Prince Ribbit, it's essential to tote your kissing gloss wherever you go.

Using your pink marker, transfer the lip pattern onto the pink felt two times. Cut out your felt lips, and glue the edges together so that there's still an opening on one side. Glue a little loop of ribbon to the open side, forming a handle. Add faux gems at the end of the loop if desired. Draw a cute little pout across the center of your lips, and add glitter highlights to make them look all glossy and shiny! Smoochilicious!

10 Steps to Using Your Kissing Gloss

1. Glance coyly around the room, pretending you do not wish to be kissed.

2. Scope out the frog of your dreams.

3. Apply Kissing Gloss.

4. Glide over to your target.

5. Gaze dreamily into his eyes.

6. For extra charm, add a quick hair flip. This should do the trick.

7. Close your eyes and pucker up.

8. Think lovely thoughts, and give him a kiss to match.

9. Enjoy. The first kiss is always the sweetest.

10. When you open your eyes, a handsome prince will stand before you.

NOTE: If a handsome prince is not standing before you, give him a couple of years. Often it takes time for frogs to grow out of their tadpole-ish ways.

How They Rate as Kissers...

Bull Frog: Very manly.

Leopard Frog: He may growl a little, but he's purr-fectly harmless.

Tree Frog: Timid but oh-so sweet.

Poison-Dart Frog: Watch out! His kiss packs a deadly punch!

Seeing Fireworks?

If you see fireworks when kissing your frog, never fear. In fact, hooray! This simply means that he's the one you've been waiting for.

What to Do When Prince Alarming Is Crushing on You

Remain calm. Most of all, remain kind, and never, ever...I mean don't even entertain the thought...of being cruel. Remember, someone else's feelings are at stake. Hopefully, in time he will get the message that the two of you were never meant to live happily ever after.

Of course, if he doesn't get the hint, you could always try to persuade him that you're not really a princess. I once tricked an entire room full of suitors into thinking I was a mountain troll by laughing with a mouthful of mashed potatoes. Boy, did I lose them quickly!

Met a Few Clunkers?

If you're anything like me, you've met a fair share of clunkers (also known as toads). Please don't fret and please, please, please don't let this build a fortress around your heart. With time, you'll be able to ascertain who is kind, loyal, and worthy.

How to Handle Unrequited Love

Oh, dear me. Sigh, sigh. Sniffle, sniffle. This one's a toughy at first. As a princess, it may be difficult to understand how anyone could possibly withstand your abundant charms. Alas, it's possible. Again, remain calm and try to be pleasant (but not sugary sweet...that's phony). Although you may feel the wrath of 5,000 fire-breathing dragons, never snub him or resort to sarcasm. After all, it's not his fault that he doesn't feel the same way about you.

Also, keep in mind that he is actually doing you a favor. Love, you see, has gobs and gobs to do with chemistry. And I don't mean the kind that includes beakers and Bunsen burners. Oh no. It's all about feeling an equal reaction...like when you both get stars in your eyes or feel your cheeks start to glow. If he doesn't feel any kind of reaction, there's no chemistry. Years from now you will look back and smile, realizing that he was indeed not the highest jumper in your pond after all...merely a passing fancy.

Who's Your Prince?

*You'll flip over this next project
...and decide which prince is for you.*

Transfer the lily pad pattern five times onto the green felt and cut them out. Glitterize your lily pads and plastic frog however you wish. If you're lucky enough to find the right shape, you can even make a flower bead into a princess hat for your pretty little froggy by pushing a snippet of netting through the hole with a straight pin. Next use your circle templates to mark a small circle (about 1¼ inch in diameter) on your yellow felt. Cut this circle out and stick a "1" on one side and a "2" on the other. Glitterize around the edges. There! Now you have your golden ball.

Her Royal Majesty Requests

- Jumping Plastic Party Frog (I found mine in pink!)
- Green Felt
- Tiny Bit of Yellow Felt
- "1" and "2" stickers (available with alphabet sticker sets)
- Small Circle Templates
- Glitter
- Flower-Shaped Bead and Tiny Snippet of Netting (optional)
- Marker
- Pink Paper
- Straight Pin
- Craft Scissors
- Craft Glue

Rules for the Game "Who's Your Prince?"

Are you ready to play "Who's Your Prince?" Good. Here's how:

✳ Cut five little pink crowns out of paper, and write the name of a boy you like on each one.

✳ Turn them over and shuffle them around a little so that you don't know which name is on which crown.

✳ Keep the papers facing down and put one crown under each lily pad.

✳ If you are playing with someone else, toss the golden ball to see who goes first. (The "1" or "2" will tell you if you're first or second.)

✳ Flip Little Miss Frog Princess and see where she lands.

✳ If she lands on a lily pad, she has found your prince!

✳ If not, just keep playing until she does....Frog princesses love to flippety-flop around even when they're not looking for princes.

And Now for a Little Amphibiance...

Music has the power to set his heart aflutter like a butterfly in springtime. Create a romantic setting for you and your sweetheart with one of these musical compositions.

Flower Duet by Leo Delibes—As enchanting as singing water lilies.

O Mio Babbino Caro ("Oh, My Dear Baby") by Giacomo Puccini—Ultra dreamy!

Barcarolle by Jacques Offenbach—Romance at its finest.

The Swan by Camille Saint-Saëns—Glistening, gliding, and feathery smooth.

The Great Gate of Kiev by Modest Petrovich Mussorgsky—He'll feel like the only prince in the world.

Water-Lily Barrettes

He'll really want to invite you over to his pad (lily pad, that is) when he sees you wearing these hair accessories. First cut green felt into a little lily-pad shape (you can copy the lily-pad template in this book and use it as a guide) and glitterize if desired. Then cut ribbon or netting into little strips and glue them close to the middle of your pad so that they resemble the petals of a water lily. Add a bead to the center of the flower for extra flair. Now glue a barrette to the back of your lily pad.

Repeat directions for more water-lily barrettes. Wait for everything to dry and put them in your hair. Triple ribbit! Be prepared to see frogs doing back flips as you glide past their pond!

Snow White

"Mirror, mirror on the wall, who's the fairest of them all?"… "What?!? Snow White?!?!" Well, that sure throws the Evil Queen for a loop. But really now, don't you feel a wee bit sorry for her? Imagine being the fairest in the land all those years and then waking up one morning only to find that you've been replaced? Poor Evil Queen! As for Snow White, looks aren't the only thing she has to offer, and I think that mirror knows it. She also has a kind heart, which in my fairy tale is the best trait of all.

"You're the Fairest of Them All" Magic Mirror

Who's the fairest of them all? Silly question! You are! Cut the crafting foam into a fancy frame that fits your mirror. Glue gems in a very royal fashion all over the frame. Then cut your sparkly paper into curvy shapes that accent your frame's edges and glue these in place (anchoring them on the back side of the frame). Set the frame aside to dry. In the meantime, write "You're the fairest of them all" in alphabet stickers at the bottom of the mirror.

Glue your fancy frame to your mirror and allow it to dry. Wow! Look at the princess in that Magic Mirror. She's not just fair—she's dazzling!

You're the fairest of them all...

WARNING: As fun as your Magic Mirror may be, a true princess does not pause in front of her reflection too often. Remember: real beauty lies within.

Her Royal Majesty Requests

- A Plain Mirror
- Enough Crafting Foam to Frame Your Mirror
- A Variety of Faux Gems
- Tiny Alphabet Stickers
- Sparkly Paper
- Scissors
- Craft Glue

Dwarfs Aplenty

When it comes to dwarfs, the more the merrier. And nothing says "dwarf" more than a hat...especially seven of them perched on the heads of your pets, brothers, or plush animals.

Enlarge the hat pattern on a photocopier to the size that will best fit your chosen dwarf. Transfer the pattern onto your fabric and cut your hat out. Fold the hat around so that the outer edges line up and a cone shape is formed. Then glue the edges together, one overlapping the other. Gently press to make sure that the glue is evenly distributed. Now glue a pom-pom at the tippy-top point of the hat. Allow 1 hour to dry. Pop this little number on your chosen dwarf. If you're feeling crafty, make six more.

＊To prevent fraying, mix a little bit of glue with a little bit of water. Then paint your hat's edges with it.

＊If you want your hat to look a little on the floppy side, fold it over a tad and tack it in place with a needle and thread.

Her Royal Majesty Requests

❧ *Colorful Fabric (Checks and polka dots are dandy for dwarfs.)*

❧ *Pom-Poms*

❧ *Marker*

❧ *Fabric Scissors*

❧ *Craft or Fabric Glue*

Gems from the Mine

If diamonds are a girl's best friend, does that make amethyst, rubies, and pink sapphires mere acquaintances? I beg to differ....A gem is a gem no matter how you cut it.

Sprinkle a fair amount of glitter into one of your empty tubs. Set aside. Take a Styrofoam ball, and, using your sponge brush, coat it completely and evenly with glue. Put the Styrofoam ball into your glitter tub and seal the lid. Do a little glitter dance while shaking the tub. When you open the tub back up, a beautiful gem will be waiting inside. Let this gem dry, and make some more. After you've made a bunch of gems and they're all dry, you can make fine jewelry.

Ritzy Ring Cut a 3-inch piece of pipe cleaner. Wrap it around your ring finger and twist the ends together. Stick the excess into one of your nice glittery gems. How perfectly splendid!

Bedazzling Bracelet Using a pipe cleaner, string three to five small gems together. Wrap it around your wrist so that there's still some room to spare. Then twist the ends together and clip off the excess. Gadzooks! It's gorgeous!

✶Remember to thank the dwarfs for putting in all that overtime in the mine to get you your gems!

Her Royal Majesty Requests

- *Small Styrofoam Balls*
- *A Variety of Glitter*
- *Gold or Silver Pipe Cleaners*
- *Wire Clippers*
- *2 or 3 Empty Butter Tubs with Lids*
- *Sponge Brush*
- *Plain Old School Glue*

Apple-of-My-Eye Locket ✦ ✦

For Little Sis, the first day of school can be almost as scary as entering a spooky forest. Show her that you care by making her an Apple-of-My-Eye Locket. Then make a matching one for yourself. There's even a pocket for the two of you to exchange secret messages.

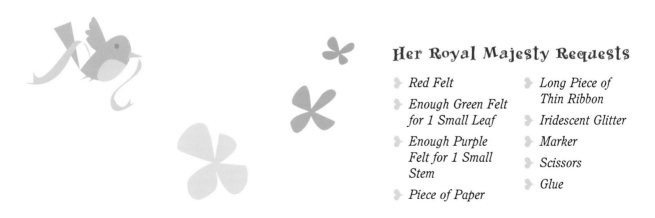

1. Transfer the apple pattern onto your red felt and cut out the 2 apples.

2. Next make a little leaf out of green felt and a stem out of purple felt.

3. Glitterize 1 apple and, if you wish, even the leaf.

4. Now turn the sparkly apple over and line the 2 sides and bottom with glue. Stick this apple to the matching side of the other felt apple to form a pocket.

5. Then glue the leaf and stem in place at the back of the locket.

6. Finally, cut ribbon to desired length and glue both ends of the ribbon neatly to the back of the leaf and stem so that you've made your little sister's locket into a pendant. Allow an hour or two to dry.

7. While you are waiting, think of some nice messages that you would like to slip inside her locket and write them down on a piece of paper. Cut out your favorite one and after the glue dries, put it in the locket pocket. If you want it to be a surprise, wrap her locket in pretty tissue paper and hide it in her lunch box.

Her Royal Majesty Requests

- Red Felt
- Enough Green Felt for 1 Small Leaf
- Enough Purple Felt for 1 Small Stem
- Piece of Paper
- Long Piece of Thin Ribbon
- Iridescent Glitter
- Marker
- Scissors
- Glue

32

Here are some ideas for sweet things that you could write to Li'l Sis:

🌸 *You're the apple of my eye!*
   (This one is predictible but very cute.)

🌸 *I will love you forever!*

🌸 *You're cute to the core!*

🌸 *I'm candy-apple sweet on you.*

Now...although these are quite nice, I'm sure that you can come up with some better ones on your own! So hop to it!

＊ Little sisters aren't the only ones who love presents. Your best friend, mom, grandmother, aunt, teacher, or even big sis might enjoy an Apple-of-My-Eye Locket.

33

Apple-Cookin' Apron

As a princess, it's important to dress for the occasion. So cook up some style with your very own adorable apron.

1. Fold your pink felt rectangle in half along the width. You will notice that 2 corners are along the crease and 2 corners now lie loose.

2. Pick one of the loose corners and use your scissors to round off the corner. When you unfold your felt, you should have a nice, symmetrical U-shape. If not, no apron for you (giggle, giggle).

3. Center your ribbon along the top (flat part) of your U-shape. Glue it in place.

4. To make your apron frilly, glue lace trim all around the edge. For pockets, cut your scraps of gingham, checkered, or plaid fabric into little rectangles or U's and glue them into place (remember to leave the top edge glue-free). Most aprons like to twinkle, so glue some faux gems on too.

Her Royal Majesty Requests

- Pink Felt Rectangle (big enough for an apron)
- 1½ Yards of Ribbon 1 to 2 Inches Wide
- Small Amount of Red and Green Felt
- Scraps of Gingham, Checkered, or Plaid Fabric
- Lace Trim
- Faux Gems
- Ultra-Fine Iridescent Glitter
- Marker
- Fabric Scissors or Good Crafting Scissors
- Glue

5. Here comes the finishing touch. Using the template from the Apple-of-My-Eye Locket, make an apple out of the red felt, a leaf out of the green felt, and a stem out of the pink scraps left over from cutting your apron. Glue everything in place on the apple and glitterize if desired.

6. When you are happy with your apple, find a fetching spot and glue it on to your apron. Wait about 2 to 3 hours for everything to dry.

Tie your apron around your waist and glide into the kitchen. Those apples are beckoning!

P.S. If you are worried about soiling your Apple-Cookin' Apron, try wearing it only for serving and not for heavy-duty cooking and baking.

Smart Apple Tart Hat

This hat's got so much attitude, people may accuse you of being a bad apple. I say, no way!...You're just one super-glad, well-clad, fashion-mad apple.

Apply glue to the area on your cap where you want the marabou to adhere. Oh-so-carefully stick it in place, making sure that the ends of the marabou are in the back of your hat. Now cut a cute little leaf shape out of your green felt and a nice little stem shape out of your purple felt. For extra glamour, glitterize the leaf and add sequins to your stem. Yippee! You're almost there. Glue that leaf and stem to the top of your cap and allow an hour or two for drying time. "A" is for apple...and adorable.

Her Royal Majesty Requests

- Red Hat (a schoolboy cap like this works well)
- Pink or Red Marabou Trim (to go around the brim)
- Green Felt (for the leaf)
- Purple Felt (for the stem)
- Pink or Purple Sequins
- Iridescent Glitter
- Glue
- Scissors

Fairy-Tale-Come-True Wishing Well

Once upon a time, wishes were granted like nobody's business. Well, times have changed, princess, so get out ye old craft supplies and make your own Fairy-Tale-Come-True Wishing Well.

Wishing Well

The well is made out of a small plastic bucket just like the ones sold at Easter time. I glued a red gingham ribbon around the top edge for extra color. The roof is just 2 identical pieces of pink matte board taped in place with clear packing tape, but you can easily use cardboard instead. For added frou-frou, I decorated the roof with red heart-shaped gems and lace trim.

Now create Woodland Flora and Fauna!

Heart Wishes To set your dreams in motion, cut colored paper into heart shapes and write your dearest wishes on them. Then wish with all your heart and cast them tenderly into the well. Here are some wishful ideas.

My fairy tale will come true when
_____.

I dream that _____

and I will someday ride off into the sunset.

I hope that _____

and I stay best friends forever.

If _____, I will live happily ever after.

Woodland Flora and Fauna

Create a whimsical woodsy wonderland by simply opening your eyes and looking at what's around you.

* Transform branches and pinecones into trees.
* Cut felt into cute animal shapes, back them with cardboard, and decorate.
* Paint and glitterize Styrofoam to use "as is" or as a base for another creation.
* Use a pretty patterned fabric as a forest floor.

Spooky Trees

Remember when Snow White ran into the forest to escape her step-mother, the Evil Queen? Well, to a young girl, the trees seemed spooky. Here you can make your own. Sure, they're ooky and kooky, but that doesn't mean they're not delicious.

ROYAL HIGHBROW INGREDIENTS

3 Cups of Cocoa Krispies Cereal

3 Cups of Pretzel Sticks

½ Cup Chocolate Chips

10.5-ounce Bag of Tiny Marshmallows

4 Tablespoons of Butter

Red Cinnamon Candies

1. Melt butter in a large saucepan over low heat. Add marshmallows (saving ½ cup for eyes) and chocolate chips. Stir until melted. When mixture is creamy smooth, remove it from the heat.

2. Immediately add cereal and pretzels, and stir until completely mixed. Allow the mixture to cool enough so that it can be touched. (This should be about 3 minutes.)

3. Coat the palm of your hands and your fingers with butter to prevent stickiness. Scoop out handful clumps of the yummy mixture and form them into tree shapes.

4. Make the trees super spooky by adding marshmallow eyes with red cinnamon-candy pupils. You may need to press hard to get the marshmallows and cinnamon candies to stick, but the eerie effect is well worth the effort.

5. Display the trees together on a dark and sinister-looking plate. Now bite into the spookiest tree you can find and enjoy. The more Spooky Trees you eat, the less frightening the forest.

Cinderella

You know the story...rags turn into a beautiful gown, the pumpkin turns into a coach, and Cinderella goes to the ball in glass slippers. But did you know this? In some versions of the tale, Cinderella may have gone to the ball in fur slippers. That's right. In French the word for glass is verre; however, the word for a certain type of pelt is vair. So...when people passed the story on, some thought "glass" while others thought "fur." The beauty of it for us is that with this newfound knowledge, you can fashion whatever kind of slippers your tootsies desire.

The Patchwork Skirt Cinderella Only Wished She Had

Cinderella thought her raggedy patchwork skirt was pathetic. Perhaps that's only because she never had this one.

Cut scraps of pretty fabric into pleasing little shapes (squares and hearts are great for patches). Lay your jean skirt onto a flat surface and plan where you want to place your patches. Now take your first patch and apply glue around the edges. Stick the patch in place and gently press down the edges. Repeat with your other patches. Then trim the bottom of your skirt with eyelet. For extra decoration, trim your patches and eyelet with rickrack, ribbon, or glitter, and allow everything to dry (overnight is best). Talk about patchwork with pizzazz! If only Cinderella had known!

Her Royal Majesty Requests

- Jean Skirt (preferably an old one)
- Scraps of Pretty Fabric
- Rickrack
- Ribbon
- Eyelet Trim
- Glitter
- Craft Scissors
- Craft or Fabric Glue

Flirty Hair Kerchief

Here's another way to have a ball while cleaning. Take a very long piece (30 inches or so) of wide ribbon and center it along the edge of a fabric triangle (that fits your head). Glue it in place. Allow at least an hour or two of drying time. Now clean in style or wear it out on the town!

Jeweled Feather Duster

If a princess must finish her chores before going out, she should at least do it with flair. With a Jeweled Feather Duster, you'll feel like the belle of the ball before you even arrive.

Decide which order you would like to put your gems, and trim on your duster. Lay them out in that order. Apply glue to the back of the first gem or snippet of trim. Place it on the feather duster. Repeat until you have the desired decoration. Finally, glue a tuft of marabou on the end. Dust away!

Her Royal Majesty Requests

- Colored Feather Duster (A flat handle works best.)
- Faux Gems
- Beaded Plastic Trim (optional)
- Tuft of Marabou
- Scissors
- Craft Glue

40

Crazy-Quilt Mousies

Fill these fashionable little mice with catnip for your kitty or potpourri to keep your slippers smelling sweet!

1. Cut 2 raindrop shapes of equal size out of felt (they should be about 3 inches long).

2. Then cut 2 mouse ears out of a different color felt. Keep those scissors in hand and cut 2 tiny little square patches out of your fabric scraps. Now that your mousie parts are all cut out, you're ready to begin gluing.

3. On one of the raindrop shapes, glue around the edges except for about an inch of space near what will be the tail. Lay the other raindrop shape directly on top of the gluey one and press down firmly. Let it dry for about an hour.

4. Now fill the little body up with a combination of either stuffing and catnip or stuffing and potpourri. When your mouse is nice and plump, glue the rear shut, adding about 4 inches of ribbon for a sleek, long tail. To make sure everything remains tightly adhered, you may want to clamp the final section together with a clothespin while it is drying.

5. Your stylish rodent friend is almost complete. Just glue on the ears, patches, and buttons for eyes and wait for about an hour. You now have either a sweetly scented sachet or a fun toy for kitty!

Her Royal Majesty Requests

- Thin Wooden Dowel or Stick
- Styrofoam Star
- Ribbon
- Iridescent Glitter
- Pearlized Acrylic Craft Paint
- Paintbrush
- Sponge Brush
- Scissors
- Plain Old School Glue

If you are worried that your kitty will be a tad too harsh on your mousie, sew on the button eyes rather than gluing them.

Flickering Fairy Godmother Wand

Every now and then a princess needs a little help of the conjuring kind. All you need is a flick of the wrist and some magic words to accompany your Fairy Godmother Wand.

First paint your dowel and star a pretty color. When everything is dry, then sponge paint your star with glue and glitterize. Add a dab of glue to the end of your dowel and stick it into your star. For the final touch, add ribbon.

It is now your own personal Flickering Fairy Godmother Wand. (Finding a fairy godmother might prove to be more difficult.)

Her Royal Majesty Requests

- Thin Wooden Dowel or Stick
- Styrofoam Star
- Ribbon
- Iridescent Glitter
- Pearlized Acrylic Craft Paint
- Paintbrush
- Sponge Brush
- Scissors
- Plain Old School Glue

To accompany your wand, here are some magic words that work wonders:

"Piff, Pang, Poof, Pop!
Brand New Ball Gown!
Chop, Chop, Chop!"

"Pumpkin Pie, Lizards, and Mice!
Some Little Glass Slippers
Would Sure Be Nice!"

"Yodel, Yodel.
I Don't Float!
Get Me Out of This Blasted Moat!"

"Midnight, 'Smidnight,
Oh, Boo-Hoo!
Please Let Me Stay Out Late with You!"

"Cheek-to-Cheek and Heart-to-Heart,
I Hope That We Will Never Part!"

Now make up some of your own!

Fancy-Prancy Dancing Slippers

Dance until dawn (or at least until midnight) in your splendiferous new slippers.

Twinkle Toes, you get to go crazy with these slippers!

Here are some ways to decorate your fabulous footwear.

* Draw hearts, stars, or polka dots with glue, and then sprinkle glitter on them.

* Glue on sequins, beads, or gems, and then glitterize the soles.

* Paint polka dots or hearts on your dancing shoes. Replace laces with ribbons, and then glue one fabric flower to the front of each shoe.

* Trim with marabou; then add on tiny pom-poms.

* Use all these suggestions at once...but with your mother, the Queen's, permission, of course!

Her Royal Majesty Requests

* Pair of Slippers, Shoes, or Even Sneakers
* Glitter
* Faux Gems
* Sequins, Beads, or Tiny Pom-Poms
* Marabou Feather Trim
* Ribbon
* Fabric Flowers
* Metallic or Pearlescent Craft Paint
* Paintbrush
* Craft Glue

Ballroom Boogie-woogie Disco Dance Floor

Perfect for showing off fancy footwork.

Place the side of the cardboard that you'll be dancing on face up. Now gussy that thing up with sticker paper that you've cut into hearts or squares (using your pencil, ruler, and scissors). Step onto the dance floor and leave those princes speechless with your cool moves.

If you don't have enough sticker paper, decorate your cardboard dance floor with paint and glitter!

Her Royal Majesty Requests

- Large Piece of Cardboard or Matte Board
- Glittery or Holographic Sticker Paper
- Pencil
- Ruler
- Scissors

Disco Ball Dazzle

Sparkling!

Sponge paint the Styrofoam ball, and wait for it to dry. Now make that ball sparkle like crazy by gluing glitter and faux gems everywhere in sight. You can stick sequins in place with pretty pearlized-head pins. When your disco ball is complete, loop the ribbon and pin it into the top (be sure to add a dab of glue to your pin so that the bond is extra strong). Hang the finished disco ball from the best spot in the room, and let it dazzle away!

✶ If your disco ball is stupendously large, you may need to hang it from a screw hook.

Her Royal Majesty Requests

- Medium or Large Styrofoam Ball
- Iridescent Glitter
- Large Sequins and Faux Gems
- 5 to 7 Inches of Ribbon
- Straight Pins and Pearlized-Head Pins
- Acrylic Craft Paint (in a bright color)
- Sponge Paintbrush
- Plain Old School Glue and Craft Glue (for heavier gluing)

Stroke-of-Midnight Clock Tower

Keep your eyes on the minute hand, or you'll turn into a pumpkin. (Ha, ha...caught ya.)

Draw a pretty frame shape on your crafting foam (or use ours as a template), and cut it out. (The frame must fit around the face of your alarm clock.) Place the rock inside your box (this will keep it weighted), and then wrap the box with pretty paper. Make 2 decorative scroll shapes (with square corners) out of crafting foam to adorn the base of your clock tower. Then cut your sticker paper into pretty swirly shapes that can be used for decoration. Plan where you want your gems and swirly shapes to go, and stick or glue them in place. Now glue your clock to the top of your box (which acts as its base or stand). Finally, glue your frame to your clock, and your scroll shapes to your tower base. It will take at least an hour for this towering creation to dry. Now set your clock to the correct time, and just for fun, arrive fashionably late.

Her Royal Majesty Requests

- *Alarm Clock*
- *Crafting Foam*
- *Rectangular Box (Clock must fit on top.)*
- *Small Rock that Fits Inside Box (Yes, I said "rock.")*
- *Wrapping Paper*
- *Glittery Sticker Paper*
- *Faux Gems*
- *Pencil*
- *Scissors*
- *Good, Strong Tape*
- *Craft Glue*

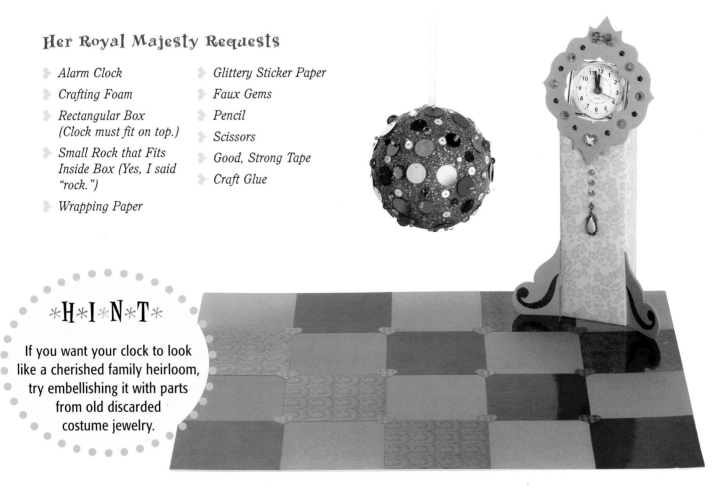

*H*I*N*T*

If you want your clock to look like a cherished family heirloom, try embellishing it with parts from old discarded costume jewelry.

45

Rapunzel

"Rapunzel, Rapunzel, let down thy hair!" Ah, if only we could grow ours that long. What a vision she is up in that tower with those golden locks cascading down. But a princess has a lot to do these days! With never-ending tresses, how would you ever manage to ride your bike, talk on your cell phone, and apply lip gloss all at once? A tangled mess is what it would be!

Dearest princess, fret no more! Rapunzel wigs and wiglets are the key. In fact, you'll have more options than she does. Transform short hair to long, straight hair to curly, or even brown hair to pink. (Yes, I said pink!) With a mane this spectacular, they'll be calling you "RaFUNzel" in no time!

Rapunzel Ribbon Wigs

Get all wigged out with ribbon wigs! You will no doubt turn heads when you walk down the street wearing this hair.

Cut the curling ribbon into very long strands (double what you want your hair length to be). Starting at the front of your net mesh cap and working your way back, loop one piece of ribbon around one section of mesh and knot it in the middle. You now have 2 long pieces of ribbon cascading down. Repeat this maneuver over and over until you feel like your fingers are going to fall off. Of course, I'm merely joking, but honestly, the more ribbon you add, the more lush and luxuriant your locks will be.

* Can't find a net mesh cap? Cut little slits in a hat, scarf, kerchief, or shower cap so that you can add your ribbon.

* If you simply must have highlights, add strands of iridescent or metallic-coated ribbon.

* Want a little more variation? Add long pieces of fabric ribbon.

* Longing for crimped hair? Add a couple clippings of rickrack.

* Do you crave curls? Holding the curling ribbon taut, run open scissors along the ribbon's edge.

* Need a trim? Get out those scissors and clip, clip, clip.

Her Royal Majesty Requests

➤ *Net Mesh Cap*
➤ *At Least 3 Large Spools of Curling Ribbon (Choose colors that go well together.)*
➤ *Scissors*

Rah-Rah Ribbon Wiglets

Get a little wiggy with ribbon wiglets! They're perfect if you don't have the time it takes to make a full wig.

Make this dandy wiglet much like the wig. Cut the ribbon to twice the desired hair length. Loop the ribbon around your ponytail band or one section of your mesh headband. Knot it in the middle so that you have two long, flowing pieces of ribbon. Repeat until you have added as much ribbon as desired. Now whip on your wiglet. Give it a quick flip, and out the door you go.

Her Royal Majesty Requests

- *Ponytail Band or Mesh Headband*
- *Scissors*
- *1 or 2 Large Spools of Curling Ribbon*

Perfectly Posh Patterned Wigs...or Wiglets!

Wear these tresses when you're on the lookout for ultra-chic, hair-raising adventure.

Follow the directions for Rapunzel Ribbon Wigs using curling ribbon. When you have attached a substantial amount of curling ribbon, repeat this process with patterned ribbon. If your ribbon happens to be the kind that is lined with wire, you can tightly roll the ends up toward the root and then gently unravel them to make big loopy curls.

Watch out world! Lady Lovely Locks is on her way!

Her Royal Majesty Requests

- *Mesh Cap or Headband*
- *At Least 2 Large Spools of Curling Ribbon*
- *Long, Wide Pieces of Patterned Ribbon*
- *Scissors*

*H*E*L*P*F*U*L*
*H*I*N*T*

If you make a super-long wig, you
may need a lady in waiting to
attend to all that hair.

A Rainbow of Rapunzels

Make Rapunzel Ribbon Wigs with all
your friends and then parade puckishly
around the neighborhood, inspiring
others with your kaleidoscopic elegance.
One of the beauties of having such
excessive hair is that you now have so
many styling options. You
know those bows, frou-
frous, and other
package decorations
that people scrap after
holidays and birthdays
(although *your* birthday
should undoubtedly be
considered a holiday
as well!)? Save them
and adorn your do till
it dazzles.

Also, remember to
shop at post-holiday
sales so that you can
scoop up discounted
ribbon and other wig-
crafting bargains. You
don't want *toupee* too
much...hee, hee, hee!

Hair Ornaments

Old-Fashioned Ribbon Barrettes

Remember, your mother, the Queen, was once a princess, too. Ask her if she wore barrettes like these when she was young. Better yet...make her a pair.

1. Cut the ribbon in half and slip it through the end of 1 unclosed barrette. Make adjustments so that the barrette is directly in the center of the ribbon.

2. Take one end of the ribbon and loop it over the top of the barrette band that it is closest to and back through the middle space to the other side.

3. Do the same with the other end of ribbon.

4. Now repeat these four steps with another color of ribbon, placing it right below the first color. Alternately loop the two different ribbons until you reach the other end of your barrette.

5. Tie all four ribbon ends into a neat knot on your barrette's underside. Cut the ribbon to an appropriate length and wear.

6. Repeat with the other barrette.

Some things are better the old-fashioned way.

Her Royal Majesty Requests

- Pair of Double-Banded Barrettes
- 1 to 2 Yards of Thin Ribbon
- Scissors
- 1 to 2 Yards of Another Color of Thin Ribbon (You must like the two colors together.)

Angel Hair

You'll be heaven-sent when you wear sheer or metallic ribbons tied in your hair.

Pom-Pom Pigtails

Pom-poms aren't just for cheerleaders. Stick them on Velcro dots and adorn your pigtails. You'll look so spirited that everyone will be cheering for you.

Bejeweled Tresses

A princess wouldn't be a princess without wearing gems in her hair from time to time. Just stick Velcro dots on the backs of a dizzying amount of jewels and get those tresses all decked out.

Bewitching Bobby Pins and Beguiling Barrettes

You know what you're doing by now. For hair with flair, glitterize either bobby pins or barrettes. Then add whatever you want, whether it's beads, felt shapes, feathers, or plastic charms. Your own personal style will be enough to lure any prince up to your tower.

How to Care for Your Own Crowning Glory

Beautiful hair comes from treating yourself well (and from good genes). Be sure to eat plenty of healthful foods, drink water like it's going out of style, and always get a good night's sleep. Here is one of Rapunzel's other secrets.

Tower-Power Hair Tonic

To have hair that's exquisite enough to cast out your tower window, try this formula.

1. Apply ¼ to ½ cup of honey to damp hair and scalp (be sure to massage it in gently).

2. Cover your hair with a disposable shower cap.

3. Wash the sticky honey off your fingers.

4. Sit for 25 to 30 minutes reading a good book.

5. Rinse hair with warm water and shampoo as you usually do.

6. Allow hair to dry naturally.

7. Sit in your tower window and let your locks shine!

Beauty and The Beast

Picture this: It's a cold and snowy winter night. Beauty's father needs shelter from the storm, so he takes refuge in the enchanted palace of the Beast. All is well until, uh-oh, he tries to sneak a single rose home for his favorite daughter.

Well, you can guess how much the Beast enjoys this little maneuver. The Beast demands that Beauty's father live with him forever unless one of his three daughters is willing to take his place. And that, my dear princess, is where our fun begins. Of course Beauty goes in his place. Of course the Beast falls in love with her. And, of course, Beauty learns that underneath all that fuzz, fluff, and fur is a heart of gold.

The Late-Bloomer Gown

Every old dress deserves a second chance to blossom, and with wire-stemmed fabric roses it's not difficult at all. Just take a long-forgotten dress that you haven't worn in ages (Mine just happened to have a rose pattern on it...wasn't I lucky?) and twist the stems of the roses around little pinches of fabric. I find that bunches of roses look mighty regal near the shoulders, waist, and hem of a dress, so don't be shy when fastening them.

Magic Rose Rings

The Beast gave Beauty a magic ring that could take her any place she wished. To make your own, simply wrap a gold pipe cleaner around your finger, twist the ends together, and snip it to the correct length. Then twist a wire-stemmed fabric rose around your ring. Snip the end if necessary. Now let your Magic Rose Ring transport you to the land of Beauty.

55

Everything's-Coming-Up-Roses Hair Garden

Ritzy ditzy! Is this a rose garden or a hairstyle? Well, both actually. Twist the same type of wire-stemmed fabric roses that you used on your Late-Bloomer Gown into your hair, and rosy elegance will blossom everywhere.

Rose-Colored Glasses

Let's face it...the world is a warmer place when viewed through rose-colored glasses. Think pink, princess!

1. If your sunglasses are not already glitterized, work your magic now.

2. Cut four equal lengths of ribbon. About 15 to 24 inches is a good length.

3. Tie two pieces around the frame near the outer corner of one of the lenses.

4. Finish with a knot.

5. Repeat this process with the other two ribbons.

6. Glue or twist (using the wire stem) fabric roses onto your sunglasses where desired.

7. Put them on and behold how rosy life looks!

Her Royal Majesty Requests

- Pink Sunglasses with Pink-Tinted Lenses
- Pink Ribbon
- Pink Fabric Roses (and a couple of yellow ones, just for variety)
- Pink Iridescent Ultra-Fine Glitter
- Craft Glue

56

Dearest Rose-Enchanted Mirror

Enchanted mirrors have a wonderful way of keeping those who are special close to us at all times. Roses and glitter make that bond even more magical.

1. Choose a photo of your best friend or a dear one. Make sure that it's OK to cut it into a shape. (You'll want to be certain that someone has a duplicate.)

2. Glue roses and leaves on your mirror in the fashion you would like them to appear. Cut the photo into a cute shape (like a flower or heart) and glue it onto your mirror. Press down firmly to smooth out any puckered areas.

3. Outline your photo with glue and add glitter.

4. Wait about 1 hour for everything to dry. If you wish, add heart stickers for extra sweetness.

5. **Painted Roses** (optional) If you want even more decoration on your Enchanted Mirror, paint the edges of your roses, or add a pretty pattern (like polka dots) to each petal.

Gaze into your Enchanted Mirror to see your reflection alongside the photo of your friend or dear one. Your mirror is telling you that, no matter what happens in life, the two of you will always be together.

Her Royal Majesty Requests

- *Vanity Mirror with Handle*
- *Fabric Roses and Leaves*
- *Heart Stickers (optional)*
- *Pearlized Acrylic Craft Paint (optional)*
- *Fine-Tip Paint Brush (optional)*
- *Iridescent Glitter*
- *Small Photo of Your Best Friend or Someone Very Dear*
- *Scissors*
- *Craft Glue*

Beast of My Dreams

What does the Beast really look like? This is entirely up to you to decide. Here you can create your own Beast mask.

To Make Leopard Print: Paint little dark pink blotches all over your pink felt. Now paint smaller hot-pink dots inside these blotches or glitterize the center of each dot.

To Make Zebra Print: Take your white felt and paint dark pink or hot-pink stripes across it. For a very sparkly zebra, add a dash of glue here and there and sprinkle on some glitter. Make sure that your stripes are not too perfect...it's very zebra-like to have them zigzag a little.

Wait for your animal print to dry. Then cut the felt into small decorative shapes to look like tufts or feathers. Here comes the really fun part. Plan out how you want your animal print, faux fur, feathers, marabou, roses, pom-poms, and ribbon to look on your mask. Then glue them on, beginning with what you have planned for the back layer first. It may take some time to adhere everything to your mask, but it will be well worth it. When your Beast mask is dry, put it on and give a loud growl. Sometimes it's fun to act a little kooky wild.

P.S. If you're brave, you can try it on a neighbor boy.

Her Royal Majesty Requests

- *Party Mask*
- *Faux Fur, Feathers, or Marabou*
- *Fabric Roses, Pom-Poms, or Ribbon*
- *Pink and/or White Felt Rectangle*
- *Ultra-Fine Glitter*
- *Pearlized Acrylic Craft Paint in Dark Pink and Hot Pink*
- *Fine-Tip Paintbrush*
- *Craft Scissors*
- *Craft Glue*
- *Plain Old School Glue (for glitterizing)*

Cascading Roses Bookmark

Beauty is a bookish princess. So it should come as no surprise that every Beauty will need a bookmark for long reads between visits with the Beast. Fun! Flowery! Fabulous!

Cut out a felt rectangle that's about 1½×5 inches. Then cut a couple of 5- to 7-inch pieces of ribbon. Glue the ribbon at the top edge of your felt so that the pieces cascade down its length. Finally, glue fabric roses all along the ribbon, and wait for them to dry. Whichever book you are reading will be much happier now that its pages can be marked in style.

Her Royal Majesty Requests

- Felt
- Ribbon
- Tiny Fabric Roses
- Scissors
- Craft Glue

Bed-of-Roses Book Jacket

Let its beauty speak volumes.

1. Open your book and put it spine up, lying flat with open pages, and measure it from the tippy-most edge of the front cover to the tippy-most edge of the back cover. Add 2¼ inches to that measurement. Then measure the book's length from top to bottom. Add ¾ to 1 inch to the length.

2. Then lay out the fabric. Using your ruler as a guide, plot out your book jacket's dimensions and mark them. Cut out the shape. (It should be square or rectangular, unless you're reading a pie.) Now fold in the front cover of the jacket by ¾ inch and glue neatly along the top and bottom edge of this section, making a little pocket. Repeat with the back cover. Coat edges with a thin layer of glue to keep them from fraying.

3. Finally, get all flowery by gluing felt or fabric roses, and glitter on the front cover for decoration. If you wish to add a little handle, do so by gluing a 1½×8-inch piece of felt to the outer edge of the back cover, and sewing a cute button to the outer edge of the front cover. Snip a little slit near the end of your handle for your button to fit through. Just for bookish charm, glue a ribbon stripe down the middle. Presto! Let your book try its fancy new jacket on for size. Oh, how smart!

Her Royal Majesty Requests

- Book about 4½×6½ inches with a ¾-inch spine
- Piece of Fabric
- Felt or Fabric Roses
- Glitter
- 1½×8-inch Piece of Felt (optional)
- Cute Button (optional)
- Needle and Thread (optional)
- Ribbon (optional)
- Ruler
- Marker
- Fabric Scissors
- Craft Glue

The Little Mermaid

Did you know that in Hans Christian Andersen's story of "The Little Mermaid," she turns into sea foam? Yes, rather than taking the life of her prince to save her own, she throws herself into the water and floats like mist up above the waves. There she becomes a daughter of the air, performing good deeds and spreading joy.

As melancholy as this tale may sound, there's an important lesson: Love isn't always easy. Now this doesn't mean you have to go hurling yourself into the ocean. Goodness no! You will find, however, that as you learn to love, there are certain sacrifices you're more than willing to make.

Scallop-Shell Top

Icing on the sponge cake!

Transfer the desired shell patterns onto your felt and cut them out. Draw scallop lines onto your shells with glue, and sprinkle with glitter. Glue sequins on for extra embellishment. Now lay out your swimsuit top. Decide where you want your scallop shells to be, and glue them in place. If you want even more razzmatazz, try these tricks.

* *Cut shells out of patterned fabric and glue them on top of your felt ones (before they are glitterized). Then decorate up a storm.*

* *Make pretty swirls and hearts out of felt and add those to your top as well.*

Attention, Bathing Beauty! This top is for poolside use only. Diving into the wild blue depths wearing felt and glitter makes an unfathomably murky mermaid!

Her Royal Majesty Requests

* *Swimsuit Top*
* *Felt Assortment*
* *Sequins*
* *Glitter*
* *Patterned Fabric (optional)*

* *Marker*
* *Craft Scissors*
* *Craft Glue*
* *Plain Glue (for glitterizing)*

Sparkling Mermaid Sequin Sarong

A mermaid without sparkling scales is like a peacock without feathers.

1. Measure the length around your waist and the length from your waist to your ankles.

2. Add about 10 to 12 inches to your waist measurement. Mark that length out along the edge of your fabric. This will be the top of your sarong, so make sure the print on your fabric is going in the right direction.

3. Then, starting at the edge where your waist measurement is marked and going down, mark your waist-to-ankle length.

4. You should have a rectangle shape. Try not to get crabby; the dry stuff is almost over. Transform your rectangle into a sarong by cutting it into a big long U-shape with tabs at the top for tying around your waist.

5. Now tack netting, ribbon, and fabric scraps around the bottom edge. For tail fins, you can also cut your fabric scraps into fish scale shapes and add them to the main part of your sarong.

6. Finally, add oceans of sequins everywhere.

Tie it around your waist and be prepared to make waves.

No-Sew Version: If using a needle and thread for you is like swimming up stream, simply attach your fabric scraps with a good, strong craft glue and use glitter rather than sewing on sequins.

Her Royal Majesty Requests

- 1 Yard of Beautiful, Shimmery Fabric
- Mermaid Scale Sequins (the hole is at the top)
- Netting
- Ribbon
- Fabric Scraps (that look like fins)
- Tape Measure
- Fabric Marker
- Fabric Scissors
- Needle and Thread

Shimmering Seaweed Boa

Is that an undersea superstar or a mermaid princess? That's what they'll say when you sashay your way across the lagoon in your Shimmering Seaweed Boa.

Cut green curling ribbon into pieces that are about 7 inches long. Tie them onto your tinsel until it is completely adorned with curling ribbon. Throw that thing on. Making a splash is such fun!

Her Royal Majesty Requests

- *5 to 7 Feet of Green or Turquoise Tinsel*
- *2 Spools of Green Curling Ribbon (Try to find 2 different greens.)*
- *Scissors*

Sea Bauble Bracelet

With coral, pearls, and sea anemone providing the decoration, this is no ordinary bauble.

Cut your felt into a variety of tiny squiggles that resemble coral and sea anemone. Glue them onto your ponytail band. Add pearl beads for the finishing touch. Now, adorn your wrist and submerge yourself in glamour...mermaid style!

Her Royal Majesty Requests

- *Stretchy Fabric Ponytail Band*
- *Brightly Colored Felt*
- *Faux Pearl Beads*
- *Scissors*
- *Craft Glue*

Twinkling Undersea Tiara

With this tiara, I crown thee goddess of the sea. Wowee!

Follow the Razzling-Dazzling Tiara directions from "The Classic Princess" chapter for your basic tiara. This time, add painted shells or starfish for decoration. Then let a tidal wave of creativity take over by gluing faux pearls and gems, sequins, shell beads, and glitter wherever you desire. Allow drying time and wear with twinkling undersea elegance. Your charm will illuminate the ocean.

Her Royal Majesty Requests

- Plain or Glitterized Headband
- 2 Pipe Cleaners
- Painted Shells or Starfish
- Faux Pearls, Faux Gems, Sequins, and Plastic Shell Beads
- Iridescent Glitter
- Wire Clippers
- Craft Glue

Clamshell Pocket Mirror

First, make sure that the scallop-shell pattern (from the Scallop-Shell Top) fits your pocket mirror. If not, enlarge the pattern. Transfer the pattern onto your felt and your pearlescent fabric two times. Then cut out your shells. Glue each pearlescent shell to a felt shell with a just little bit of overlap showing. Next add lines of glitter for scallops and sequins for decoration. Then adorn each side of your pocket mirror with a shell, making sure it can open and close with ease. Allow drying time.

Now find a pretty rock to sit on and gaze into your reflection as storybook mermaids often do. Just try not to be too showy about it!

Her Royal Majesty Requests

- Small Pocket Mirror
- Felt Rectangle
- Pearlescent or Shimmery Fabric
- Sequins
- Glitter
- Scissors
- Craft Glue (if you like a thinner glue for glitterizing, have that on hand, too.)

Terrifying Pink Tiger-Shark Headband

People will swim for their lives when they see you wearing this creation!

Cut crafting foam into 2 small shark fin shapes (basically a triangle with a slight curve to it) that will look just right perched on top of your head, and glue them together.

Wait about an hour for drying time and then, with a hot-pink marker, draw some snazzy tiger-shark stripes on either side. For shimmer, draw a line of glue inside each tiger stripe and glitterize.

When the glitter has adhered, glue your shark fin to the headband. To keep your shark fin in place while drying, try anchoring it with tape. Once your headband has dried, put it on and accessorize further with a nice toothy smile. I do declare, isn't it fun to be the most powerful creature in the ocean?!

Crafty Tidbit: I chose to use a rippling blue headband because it looks like waves. If you want your shark fin to be extra secure, however, you may want to choose a thicker one. You may also want to keep your shark fin taped on if you expect to be out patrolling extra stormy seas.

Her Royal Majesty Requests

- *Plain or Glitterized Headband*
- *Sheet of Pink Crafting Foam*
- *Hot-Pink Marker*
- *Light Pink Glitter*
- *Paper*
- *Glue*
- *Tape*
- *Scissors*

CAUTION: Not for use in water. We here at the Princess Institute do not wish to be held responsible for the frightful misunderstandings that may occur if you attempt to swim while wearing your Terrifying Pink Tiger-Shark Headband.

Mermaid Waves

Mermaids love to wear their hair in waves that rival the ocean, and well, who wouldn't? To wear your hair this way, wash and braid it before going to bed. When you wake up, undo the braids and voila! Of course, if you already have wavy or curly hair, you don't need our help. Flaunt it!

Sly-but-Sweet Sea Horse Pocketbook

Sea horse daddies are awfully sweet. They carry their babies around in a secret pouch to make sure they're safe and sound. Now, you too can keep tiny treasures protected with your very own Sly-but-Sweet Sea Horse Pocketbook (secret pouch included).

1. Transfer the sea horse and secret pouch templates from this book onto the green felt.

2. When cutting out your shapes, you will more than likely have a dickens of a time when you get to the sea horse's tail. Don't give up. Cut nice and slowly and turn your felt as you go along. Yippee! You did it! Then measure out a 4×5½-inch rectangle on your turquoise felt. Repeat this step so that you have two rectangles. Cut them both out. If you wish, cut a slight curve around each edge to soften the angle.

3. Now take your sheer ribbon and determine how long you want your handle to be. Your turquoise and green ribbon will act as fringe, so cut these to a desired length.

4. Here's another slightly tricky step. Lay one of your turquoise felt rectangles down on a nice flat surface, and glue your handle in place at the top and your fringe in place at the bottom. Then, starting at the top, glue down the length of one side, across the bottom width and up the length of the other side. Now lay your other turquoise felt rectangle neatly on top of the one with glue. Press down around the edges to ensure a nice strong bond.

Her Royal Majesty Requests

- Green Felt Rectangle
- Turquoise Felt Rectangle
- Small Amount of White Felt
- Faux Gem
- Sequins
- Iridescent Ultra-Fine Glitter
- Piece of ½-inch-wide Sheer Ribbon
- Assorted Pieces of Turquoise and Green Ribbon
- Turquoise or Green Marker
- Ruler
- Good Crafting Scissors
- Circle Template (optional)
- Plain Old School Glue

5. While your pocketbook is drying, use your circle template to make bubbles on your white felt. If you don't have a circle template, trace around something round like the bottom of a bottle of nail polish. Cut out your bubbles, line the edges with glue, and glitterize.

6. Line the edges of your sea horse with glue and add a dash or two of glitter. Do the same with your secret pouch (be sure to decorate the side that will be showing). If you want glitter anywhere else, now is the time to add it. When you have amply glitterized, flip your pouch over and line all the edges except for the top one with glue. Quickly stick your pouch onto your sea horse.

7. For the finishing decorative touch, add a faux gem for an eye and sequins for extra sparkle. Now decide where to place your sea horse and bubbles on your pocketbook and glue them in place. When all is dry, take your Sly-but-Sweet Sea Horse Pocketbook out for a day at the aquarium.

Extra Special Reminder: Practice makes perfect! The better your cutting skills, the more crafting options you will have!

Fish-Bone Comb

Who doesn't need one?

Lay your comb onto your vinyl or felt, and draw a funky fish shape around it. Cut out your fish shape. Then cut an area in the middle that will allow your comb to fit. Glue your fish around the edge of your comb. Add sticker paper and sequins for eyes, fins, and extra frills. Allow glue to dry (you wouldn't want sticky hair) and comb those beautiful tresses.

Her Royal Majesty Requests

- Comb
- Clear Vinyl or Felt
- Glittery Sticker Paper
- Sequins
- Marker
- Scissors
- Craft Glue

Hawaiian Princess

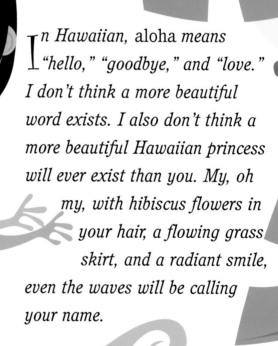

In Hawaiian, aloha *means* "hello," "goodbye," *and* "love." *I don't think a more beautiful word exists. I also don't think a more beautiful Hawaiian princess will ever exist than you. My, oh my, with hibiscus flowers in your hair, a flowing grass skirt, and a radiant smile, even the waves will be calling your name.*

Hula-La Skirt!

Here's a grass skirt to groove in.

1. Make sure the fabric ribbon ties in a bow around your waist with some to spare. About 10 inches from the end of the ribbon, tie a knot.

2. Using the curling ribbon, measure how long you want your grass skirt to be. Double that length and cut. This piece will be your guide for cutting the other pieces.

3. After you have a couple of pieces precut, take one and fold it in half, making a crease. Tie this piece around the fabric ribbon at a point just in from where you have made your knot. Tie another curling ribbon next to the first one.

4. Continue this process until you have tied enough curling ribbon to complete a grass skirt. Tie a knot in your fabric ribbon at this point as well.

Put on your hula skirt by tying a bow and then shifting the bow to your back. Now get all groovy in your new grass skirt. Wear it over some shorts or capri pants.

Grass Skirt in a Breeze: If you're crunched for time just buy thicker ribbon. Fabric is lovely also. That way, the skirt will look full more quickly.

Her Royal Majesty Requests

- 1 Long Thin Piece of Fabric Ribbon (It must tie comfortably around your waist.)
- Loads of Curling Ribbon (grassy strands)
- Scissors

Aloha Flower Lei

Say "hello" Hawaiian style. In fact, this lei is so gorgeous that you can simply let the flowers do the talking.

Cut the felt into 2- to 3-inch squares. (They don't have to be exact.) Then cut the squares into pretty flower shapes. Do the same with your netting. Measure out at least 65 inches of thread so that you have plenty of extra. Thread your needle, and tie the two ends into a good, sturdy knot. Move your needle to the end opposite your knot. Now for the fun part...randomly thread your flowers, pom-poms, beads, and sequins. Make sure you give all your crafty materials a chance to shine. When your lei is at the length you want, cut the needle off the thread and tie the two ends of thread together. (It's a good idea to double or triple the knot.) Your flower lei is ready to say "aloha"!

Glitterized Variation: Fill a clean, empty butter tub with glitter. Using plain old school glue, add polka dots to a large pom-pom or felt flower. Then place it in the tub and seal the lid. Shake it about and unseal. Your pom-pom is all glitterized! Repeat this process with as many pom-poms or flowers as you wish.

Her Royal Majesty Requests

- *2 Felt Rectangles in Hot Tropical Colors*
- *Sparkle Netting*
- *Variety of Sparkle Pom-Poms*
- *Variety of Beads and Sequins*
- *Beadable Pom-Poms (if available)*
- *Scissors*
- *Needle and Strong Thread (like the kind used for coats and such)*

Hibiscus Hair Ornaments

No Hawaiian princess is complete without breath-taking tropical flowers in her hair.

Transfer the hibiscus flower pattern onto your pink or red felt with a marker and carefully cut it out. Then cut two tiny vertical slits in the middle of your flower. Attach the top prong of your bobby pin to the hibiscus through these two slits. Then take your small yellow felt square and cut slits along the edge, making fringe. Bunch it up a tad so that the fringe flares out and glue it to the middle of your flower. You're almost there. All your hibiscus needs now is adequate glitter. So add a little sparkle and wear it in your hair (behind one ear looks very Hawaiian).

Fancy Variation: To create a flouncier flower, make a slightly smaller hibiscus shape out of netting and attach it to the middle of the felt hibiscus when securing the bobby pin.

Her Royal Majesty Requests

- Pink or Red Felt Rectangle
- 2 to 3 Square Inches of Yellow Felt
- Sparkle Netting (optional)
- Glitter
- Bobby Pin
- Marker
- Scissors
- Craft Glue

Wave-to-the-Sunset Hula Wristlet

This is just what you need for accessorizing graceful hula moves.

Cut the ribbons into oodles of 3- to 4-inch pieces. Loop one piece of ribbon around the mesh section of your ponytail band and knot it in the middle. Continue this process until you have a flowery hula wristlet.

* For an extra luscious Hula Wristlet, use ribbon in a variety of colors that work well together such as hot pink, gold, and orange.

Her Royal Majesty Requests

- Mesh Ponytail Band
- At Least 1 Spool of Curling Ribbon
- Scissors

Flower-Wow Flip-Flops

Most flip-flops are so pedestrian...but not these! Your feet will thank you. Trust me.

Trace a small hibiscus pattern onto your felt with a marker twice, or create your own flower design. Cut out the flower shapes. Draw one tiny line (about ¼ inch) horizontally in the middle of your flowers. Draw another right below it. Using these lines as a guide, make two little snips with your scissors. Add glitter where necessary. Cut two 12-inch or so pieces of curling ribbon. Attach the flower to your flip-flop by threading one piece of curling ribbon through the slits so that it ties in the front. Use scissors to curl your ribbon. Repeat with the other flip-flop. Step out and take a little Polynesian promenade to the nearest volcano! Flippety-flop, flippety-flop-flop! Look at Princess go!

Her Royal Majesty Requests

- Pair of Flip-Flops
- Tropical-Colored Felt Rectangle
- Curling Ribbon
- Glitter
- Marker
- Scissors
- Glue

How to Hula Like a Hawaiian Princess

The key to lovely hula dancing is practice. Rather than just wiggling around like a wild boar stepping on hot lava, take a hula hoop and try to balance and rotate it around your hips at the same time. This way your movement will become more fluid. As you grow better and better, add a little arm movement. To get an idea of how hula dancers hold their arms, check out a travel book on Hawaii or rent a video featuring hula dancers. You will be the picture of hula perfection in no time.

Teeny-Tiny Tiki Pendant

Oh, what tiki chic! Once you put this baby on, you may never want to take it off. Just so that you know, a tiki is a wooden or stone image of a Polynesian supernatural power.

1. In a small bowl, stir the salt and water together until the salt is dissolved.

2. Add the flour, and for best results, mush it together with your hands.

3. Knead the dough and roll it into a ball.

4. Chill the dough for 20 minutes.

5. Pinch off a piece of chilled dough that is about an inch thick. Form this piece into a little tiki shape (basically a cylinder). Save the excess tiki dough in the freezer.

6. Gently place your tiki on a cookie sheet and bake at 200°F for 1 to 2 hours.

7. When your tiki is dry and hard, take it out of the oven. Let the tiki cool down.

Now for the decorating! First paint your tiki a pretty base color. Then add a super-cute little face, using faux gems. Add glittery sticker paper for extra decoration. Glue your ribbon to the back of your tiki, and just to be romantic, tuck a tiny fabric flower behind her (imaginary) ear. Tikirrific! This will soon become a signature piece in your accessory collection.

Her Royal Majesty Requests

- *1 Cup of All-Purpose Flour*
- *½ Cup of Salt*
- *½ Cup of Warm Water*
- *Glittery Sticker Paper*
- *Faux Gems or Sequins*
- *Tiny Fabric Flower*
- *Acrylic Craft Paint*
- *Paintbrush*
- *Ribbon (long enough to make a pendant cord)*
- *Scissors*
- *Craft Glue*

Penny-Wise Hula Piggy

Saving up for a Hawaiian vacation can be a royal pain...but not with Penny-Wise Hula Piggy! She's incontestable proof that some things are worth waiting for.

Cut your felt into a 1- to 2-inch-wide strip that wraps all the way around your piggy's waist. Then cut the strip into fringe by making a series of little slits with your scissors. When your strip is all fringy, cut it in half. If you want sparkles, glitterize. Glue one strip to half of your bank and the remaining strip to the other. Your piggy is now wearing a grass skirt. Make her extra hula-worthy by gluing a flower behind her ear and buttons, beads, or sequins for eyes. Now save!

Her Royal Majesty Requests

- Piggy Bank
- Fabric Flower
- Felt
- Glitter
- Buttons, Beads, or Sequins
- Scissors
- Craft Glue

Tropical Tiki Tumblers

No tropical drink tastes as scrumptious as when it is sipped from a Tropical Tiki Tumbler. If you look quickly enough, you might even catch your tumbler winking as if to say, "Yep, this is one delicious drink."

Make up a cute little tiki face and transfer it onto your sticker paper. Neatly cut out the face shapes. Stick them onto your tumbler starting with the nose first so that you have everything centered. Press down on the tiki face so that it adheres well. Thirsty yet?

For Fancy Straws: Cut flower shapes out of shiny colored foil, and then cut a small ✕ in the middle to push your straw through.

Her Royal Majesty Requests

- Brightly Colored Plastic Tumbler
- Shiny, Glittery Sticker Paper
- Pen or Pencil
- Paper
- Scissors

Beautiful Birds of Paradise

Every Hawaiian princess needs a fine-feathered friend, and it's a well-known fact that all craft-store sparrows, chickadees, and hummingbirds are really Beautiful Birds of Paradise waiting to be transformed.

First, take your bird and glue on extra feathers (the wings and tail are usually good places for this). Allow about 1 hour to dry. Your fowl little pal is now ready for even more glamour. Here are some options:

❀ *Paint polka dots, feathery waves, or a pattern of your own on your bird.*

❀ *Embellish with sequins, pom-poms, or flowers.*

❀ *Cut netting or sheer fabric into extra feather shapes.*

❀ *Using your scissors (or a specialty shape puncher), cut little hearts, diamonds, or dots out of sticker paper, and apply them wherever you feel fit.*

❀ *Glitterize like there's no tomorrow.*

❀ *Don't feel bashful about adding as much embellishment as you want. Birds love getting all dolled up.*

Her Royal Majesty Requests

❧ *1 to 3 Craft Store Birds*
❧ *Colorful Feathers or Marabou Tufts*
❧ *Scissors*
❧ *Craft Glue*

Some or All of These:
❧ *Sequins*
❧ *Tiny Pom-Poms*
❧ *Tiny Fabric Flowers*
❧ *Shiny, Glittery Sticker Paper*

❧ *Colorful Netting or Sheer Fabric*
❧ *Glitter*
❧ *Pearlized Acrylic Craft Paint*
❧ *Fine-Tip Paintbrush*

Sleeping Beauty and Friends

Bedtime doesn't have to be boring...just take it from the Sleeping Princesses. In "The Princess and the Pea," our heroine gets to sleep on countless mattresses and is so delicate that she still feels that pesky pea under the very bottom one. Sleeping Beauty snoozes away for a hundred years and is then awakened by the kiss of her true love. (That must have been some kiss!) Last, but indeed not least, the Twelve Dancing Princesses are supposed to be all snuggled up in their beds but go out dancing instead. These gals really know how to make bedtime a blast.

Throw a Princess Pajama Party!

Invite five or so of your favorite friends and sleep under the stars. After all, it's your royal obligation to entertain princesses from far-off lands.

Royal Midnight Snack Featuring...

The Princess and the Pea Sandwich

A magnificent, mouth-watering creation indeed.

ROYAL HIGHBROW INGREDIENTS

2 Pieces of White Bread

4 Pieces of Lettuce

4 Slices of Cheese (Any Variety)

4 Slices of Lunch Meat (Any Variety)

4 Tomato Slices

8 Cucumber Slices

8 Pickle Slices

2 Teaspoons of Mayonnaise

1 Pea

1. Lay one piece of bread out on a cutting board or plate.

2. Spread 1 teaspoon of mayonnaise evenly across the surface.

3. Then stack ingredients mattress-style onto bread in this order: 1 piece lettuce, 1 slice cheese, 1 slice lunch meat, 1 tomato slice, 2 cucumber slices, 2 pickle slices.

4. three times, however, at some point during the process randomly throw in the 1 pea.

5. When stacking is complete, spread mayonnaise across the other piece of bread and lay it on top of your towering, yummy creation.

7. Now gently spin the sandwich around seven times to enchant it.

7. Cut it in half and then in half again.

8. Share the mini-sandwiches with your friends.

9. The girl who receives the pea in her sandwich gets to be the real princess for the evening!

Cloud-Nine Princess Popcorn ⭐

So light and fluffy, this scrumptious stuff belongs in the sky! Just sprinkle light blue- or pink-colored sugar on top of a batch of popped and buttered popcorn. Then add as many tiny marshmallows as you wish and mix it all together.

Sweet-Dreams Sleeping Potions ⭐

How nice it is to doze off to dreamland after a hard day of lollygagging about the castle. This formula will send you off snoozing in no time:

$1/4$ Cup Syrup + 1 Cup Milk = Super Sweet Dreams!

The syrup you choose will determine the type of dream you have!

Blueberry = Friendship
Raspberry = Your Future
Strawberry = Prince Oh-So-Charming
Blackberry = Your Innermost Secrets

Sleeping Bunny Slippers

Hoppity-hop on over to bed with these dozing beauties.

1. First, cut 4 bunny ears out of colored felt that are in proportion with your slippers. Glitterize the middle of the bunny ears if desired. Then cut the white felt into 2 little sets of bunny teeth.

2. Now pick where you want the bunny's eyelashes to go on your slippers and stick them in place.

3. You already have the bunny's ears and teeth made, so now use the large pom-poms for cheeks and small pom-poms for noses. Arrange your two bunny faces, and glue everything in place.

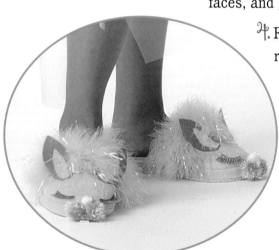

4. Finally, trim with marabou, remembering to cut and glue a tiny little fluffy tail at the back of each slipper. Cute, cute, cute! Behold bedtime charm at its best!

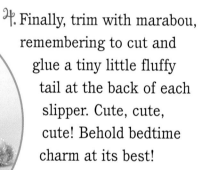

Her Royal Majesty Requests

- *Fluffy Slippers*
- *2 Sets of False Eyelashes (sparkly if possible)*
- *Marabou Trim (for trim and tails)*
- *Enough Colored Felt for 4 Ears*
- *Tiny Bit of White Felt (for teeth)*

- *4 Large Pom-poms*
- *2 Small Pom-poms*
- *Iridescent Glitter (optional)*
- *Marker*
- *Glue*
- *Craft Scissors*

Starry-Eyed Sleeping Mask

OK, so you don't get one hundred years of beauty rest, and an endless stack of mattresses is out of the question. That doesn't mean you can't sleep in style. Just put on this stellar sleeping mask, and you'll see stars in no time.

Transfer the sleeping mask template onto your felt with a marker. Cut out your pattern. Neatly write "Princess" on the face of your mask with alphabet stickers and press down to secure them firmly. Option 2 is to draw eyelashes with glue and then sprinkle them with ultra-fine glitter. Let your eyelashes dry and remove the excess glitter. Now glue one piece of ribbon to the back edge of one side of your mask. Repeat on the other back edge with the other ribbon. Allow about an hour for drying time. Your mask now is finished and, golly-gee, will the moon ever be jealous!

＊ If you wish to write "Princess" or "HRH" (Her Royal Highness) in glitter glue instead of alphabet stickers, go right ahead.

＊ Also, it's important to use ultra-fine glitter because that kind that won't irritate your face.

Her Royal Majesty Requests

- Felt
- 2 Long Pieces of Ribbon (about 24 inches each)
- Iridescent Ultra-Fine Glitter (the kind used for make-up) or Alphabet Stickers
- Marker
- Scissors
- Glue

Oh-So-Dreamy Princess Phone

Ring, ring...ring, ring..."Is Princess home?" If so, you'll want to gab, gush, and babble all night on this fancy phone!

Sponge paint your phone with pretty pearlized paint. Then doll it up by gluing glitter, gems, and fabric frillies where best suited. Add the crowning touch by trimming the base with lace or marabou and tying 7-inch pieces of netting to the cord. Now call your best bud and talk until the stars go to sleep!

Her Royal Majesty Requests

- Old Phone (white preferably)
- Pearlescent Acrylic Craft Paint (you can use a variety of shades)
- Faux Gems
- Fabric Frillies like Butterflies, Leaves, and Flowers
- Glitter
- Lace or Marabou Trim
- Netting
- Natural Sponge
- Scissors
- Craft Glue

Chatter Bag (for your cell phone, silly!)

If you're a chatter box, then this chatter bag is for you!

Measure and cut the felt into a 3×10-inch piece. (If this size is too small for your cell phone, adjust the dimensions accordingly.) Fold it in half so that it is 3×5 inches, and glue each of the two longer sides together. If necessary, place a heavy book on top while the two sides are adhering. You now have a little pocket to which you can simply add ribbon or sparkly trim for a handle. Decorate in a heavenly fashion using your beads, buttons, and sequins. Chatter, chatter, chatter, *chica*!

Her Royal Majesty Requests

- Felt Rectangle
- Sparkly Trim or Ribbon
- Beads, Buttons, and Sequins (stars and moons, if possible)
- Marker
- Ruler
- Scissors
- Craft Glue

Star-Bright Night-Light

So simple yet so radiant. Decorate a plain night-light with stickers, pom-poms, sequins, feathers, and other fun stuff. Shine on through the night.

Sleeping Beauty's Glow-in-the-Dark Manicure

Carefully pour a fair amount of glow-in-the-dark glitter into a bottle of clear nail polish. Shake well. Paint your nails and glow...after all, you want your prince to be able to find you in the dark.

Dancing Princess Marabou Slippers

Cut 2 pieces of marabou so that each one spans the width of a slipper. Attach 1 piece to each slipper by tacking it in place with a needle and thread or adhering it with a good craft glue. Now dance the night away or get ready for bed. You pick.

Toothbrush Glam

Tie colorful curling ribbon to the end of your toothbrush. For extra fun tie on glow-in-the-dark pom-poms. Brush those dazzling whites.

Flouncy Fairy Skirts

Light as air, these skirts are made for dancin'. They're easy to make too! Just take 2 yards of netting and fold it in half lengthwise over a 2-yard piece of ribbon. Now tie the ribbon around your waist and move the bow to the back. Your Flouncy Fairy Skirt will be a tad bunchy in places, so shift the netting around until it is evenly distributed. That was fairy simple, wasn't it?

84

Heavenly Hair Laurel

For a dash of celestial style, try Heavenly Hair Laurel. First, encircle metallic star garland around the crown of your head two times and cut off this length with wire clippers. Then twist the ends together so that you have a wreath shape. To decorate, tie long pieces of sheer ribbon (and some satin ribbon as well) around your laurel. For extra frills, twist wire-stemmed fabric butterflies, leaves, and flowers here and there, and trim off the excess wire. Ta-da!

Fairy Hair

To achieve the natural look that fairies go for, glue fabric leaves to the ends of ribbons and tie them in your hair. For super-duper natural charm, add fabric flowers and butterflies.

"Charmed I'm Sure" Jingle Bracelet

It's fun to jingle as you go along your merry fairy way. Make this jazzy jangler by loosely wrapping a piece of metallic star garland once or twice around your wrist and twisting the ends together. Remove the bracelet from your wrist and snip off the excess garland with a wire clipper. Then thread long strands of sheer ribbon through jingle bells and tie them all around your bracelet. It's so charming, it's disarming!

Dancing-on-Clouds Fairy Wings

Twirl through the sky like a ballerina sent by the stars. You may need help from a fairy godmother for this one.

1. Open up a grocery bag and lay it flat on the ground. Flip through your nature book until you find a picture of a butterfly that tickles your fancy. On one of the larger rectangles of the open bag, draw a big fairy wing using your picture as inspiration. If you don't like the first one you draw, erase it and try again.

2. To make sure the wing is the right size, hold it up slightly behind your back while looking in a mirror. When you have completed the outline of your wing, draw one or two shapes in the middle that echo that outline. Take care that there is at least 1½ inches of wing space between these shapes and the edge.

3. Next cut out your wing pattern (saving the middle shapes) and lay it on top of the crafting foam. Be sure it is placed so that you get maximum use out of your foam. Carefully trace around it with your marker (remember to trace the middle sections as well). Repeat 3 times so that you have a grand total of 4 wings.

4. Take the middle shapes that you saved when cutting out your wings and use them as guides for making panels out of netting or translucent gift wrap. These panels must be a little larger than the actual shape so that they can be glued in place.

5. Now lay 2 of your wings down on a flat surface (have them facing inward, toward each other, making a butterfly shape).

Put your panels in place by lining the edges of the section where they are about to fit with craft glue and then sticking them delicately onto that section. Flickering lightning bugs! It's as if you were making little windowpanes! When all of your panels are in place, glue the other 2 wings so that they fit directly on top of the ones holding your panels (like a fairy wing sandwich).

6. Tuckered out? Hang in there! Next cut 2 big raindrop shapes (at least 1½ inches wide and 2 inches long) out of your remaining scraps of crafting foam. If your wings have shifted, place them back together so that the 2 inner edges are touching each other (again making a butterfly shape).

7. Join the wings together by gluing one teardrop shape over the 2 adjoining edges in the front and the other teardrop over the 2 adjoining edges in the back. This way you will be using the teardrops as decorative anchors. (It doesn't matter whether they point up or down...they will still look nice and dainty.)

8. No need to get fidgety! You're almost done! Adorn those wings with gems and glitter. Some butterflies have details that resemble latticework, so you may even want to take another peek at your nature book to get ideas. When every last sprinkle of sparkle is in place, put your wings in a safe place to dry overnight (or at least for a very long nap).

9. In the morning, cut 2 horizontal slits (about 4 inches apart from each other vertically) on the inner section of each wing, making a total of 4 slits. Now loop a long ribbon (about 40 inches or so) through one set of slits and then another ribbon through the other. You should now have 2 little straps. Adjust each strap to the right length and tie in place with a bow. Prepare for takeoff, you flighty fairy!

Her Royal Majesty Requests

- 2 to 4 Sheets of Crafting Foam (depending on how big you want your wings)
- Netting or Translucent Gift Wrap
- Glitter (all kinds work for this project)
- Faux Gems

- ½- to 1-inch-wide Ribbon (sheer looks best)
- Nature Book with Drawings or Photos of Butterflies
- Pencil
- Marker
- Large Paper Grocery Bag

- Scissors
- Good Strong Craft Glue (for holding your wings together)
- Plain Old School Glue (for glitterizing)

Life-of-the-Party Pixie Dust ★

When I sprinkle pixie dust, I feel like I'm sprinkling baby stars. Here are some ways to make your own.

✳ Save excess glitter from other craft projects and then mix it together to create your own personalized pixie dust blend.

✳ Cut metallic curling ribbon into little tiny snippets that can be tossed in the air like confetti.

✳ Use a specialty paper puncher to make shapes like stars and hearts that can be added to your pixie mix.

✳ Combine prepackaged confetti with pretty sequins.

Pizzazzy-Dazzy Pixie Dust Locket ★ ★

Of course, you'll need a place to store all your Life-of-the-Party Pixie Dust. Some vials come with a little plastic loop through which you can thread a ribbon to make a pendant. If you do not have a vial like this, however, you can take a really long piece of ribbon and tie it tightly around the vial (near the top) remembering to add a nice strong knot. Then decorate your newly fashioned locket with glittery sticker paper and glow-in-the-dark star labels. When you are satisfied with your embellishments, add a couple pinches of Life-of-the-Party Pixie Dust to your locket. Now it is time to use your fairy intuition. Sprinkle up a storm whenever you feel the situation calls for it (like right in the middle of a big final exam or while you're waiting to be picked for a team in gym class).

WARNING: The Queen may not find Life-of-the-Party Pixie Dust as enchanting as you do, especially when vacuuming, so be sure to use it wisely and only in a place where it can be easily cleaned up.

Secret Wish Journal

Have you ever wished upon a star? Did you tell anyone? Of course not! Some things are better kept a secret.

First, cut all sorts of swirly celestial shapes out of sticker paper. Then adhere them, along with star stickers, to the cover of your journal. Stars love to sparkle, so glitterize! To jazz up your pen, glue a tuft of marabou and some gems to the cap. Finally, keep your journal in a secret place and take it out only when it's time to dream. The best part is that you get to write whatever you want, and no one will ever know.

Here are some starters:

When I finally catch that shooting star, I will wish for

_____.

My dreamiest moment was when _____.

My friends say I'm a dreamer because _____.

I'm on cloud nine when _____.

P.S. Don't be afraid of being too sappy. This journal is yours and yours alone.

Her Royal Majesty Requests

- *Journal with Black Pages (the smaller the cuter)*
- *Metallic Pen*
- *Glow-in-the-Dark Star Stickers*
- *Glittery Sticker Paper*
- *Glow-in-the-Dark Glitter*
- *Tuft of Marabou*
- *Tiny Faux Gems*
- *Scissors*
- *Craft Glue*

Heavenly Scent Princess Pillow ★ ★

Catch as many ZZZ's as you please with this pillow. It's even scented for extra sweet dreams.

1. Make a pattern out of paper and cut 1 piece of felt into a stunning celestial shape (like a star, moon, or cloud) or a classic square or rectangle. Trace this shape onto your other piece of felt and cut it out as well. Choose a piece for the front of your pillow, and using stickers, write something super-princessy (see below).

2. Make sure the letters are neatly spaced because the next step is to dab each one with a tiny bit of glue. After you have done this, immediately sprinkle glitter on top of your letters. Save the excess; wastefulness is not a good habit for a princess to fall into.

3. Glue your trim to the front pillow panel. If necessary, place a heavy book on top of the panel and trim while the two materials are adhering.

4. Then scent your stuffing by mixing it with about half a handful of potpourri. Set the freshly scented stuffing aside, and glue the edges of your front and back panels together, leaving a small gap for filling your pillow. Allow at least an hour for it to dry.

5. Stuff your pillow, and glue the remaining gap. If need be, use a clothespin to keep the gap shut while the glue is drying. Place on your bed and let the heavenly scent take you to the stars.

Her Royal Majesty Requests

- At Least 2 Felt Rectangles
- Ribbon, Lace, or Eyelet Trim
- Stuffing or Fiber Fill of Some Sort
- Potpourri (Lavender, rose, or lily-of-the-valley are very soothing.)

- Tiny Alphabet Stickers
- Iridescent Ultra-Fine Glitter
- Marker
- Paper
- Scissors
- Craft Glue
- Plain Glue (for glitterizing)

Fanciful words for pillow talk:

"Once Upon a Time..."
"Princess"
"Sweet Dreams!"
"Kiss Me! I'm a Princess!"
"If the Tiara Fits, Wear It."
"Happily Ever After"

Proper Princess Etiquette

Remember, people depend on princesses to set a good example.

* *When it comes to mirrors, a true princess never pauses too long in front of her own reflection. Real beauty lies within.*

* *If what you have to say will cause pain to someone else, it's not worth saying.*

* *If you do goof up royally and act like a complete troll, apologize at once.*

* *Keep your chin pointed toward the sunshine and smile radiantly wherever you go.*

* *Remember that life is not always peaches and cream. Sometimes even princesses have to struggle a little, but out of that struggle come compassion, kindness, and wisdom.*

* *Try to find good everywhere. The rain that soggies up your slippers also makes flowers grow.*

* *If your prince turns out to be a toad, just throw him back in the water and move on to the next pond.*

* *Let others sing your praises; pompous windbags are so tedious.*

* *When throwing your hair out the tower window, first look to see who's down below.*

* *For perfect posture, return borrowed books by walking to the library with them stacked on top of your head.*

* *Don't be deceived by a beastish facade, someone wonderful may be waiting on the inside.*

* *Never snub the 13th fairy. She may be a bit odd, but that's no excuse.*

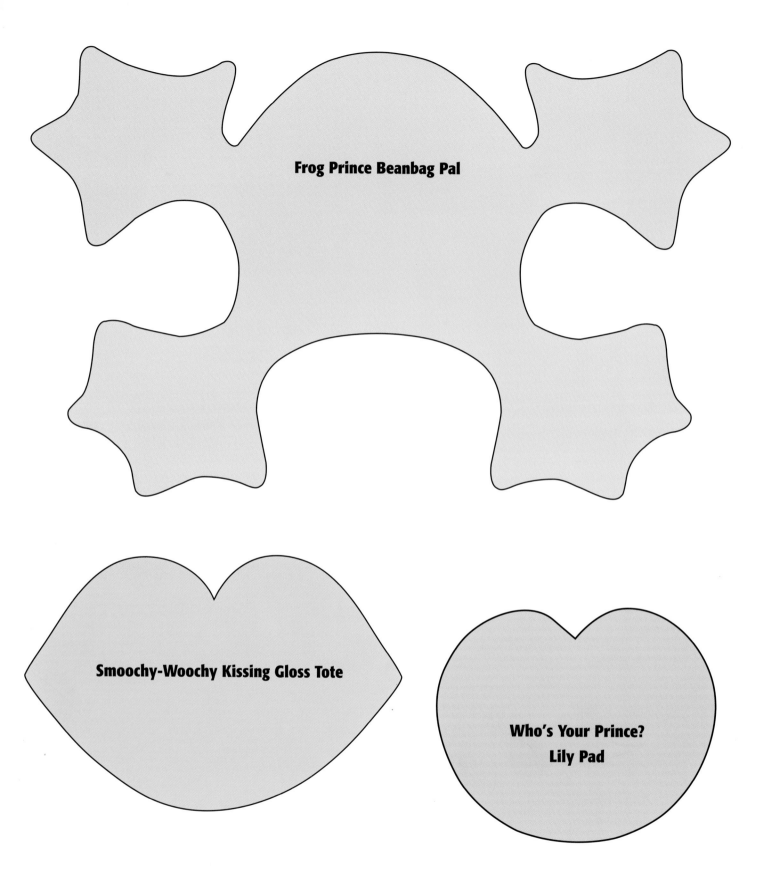

Frog Prince Beanbag Pal

Smoochy-Woochy Kissing Gloss Tote

**Who's Your Prince?
Lily Pad**

Apple-of-My-Eye Locket

Water-Lily Barrettes

Sly-but-Sweet Sea Horse

Stroke-of-Midnight Clock Tower

Secret Pouch

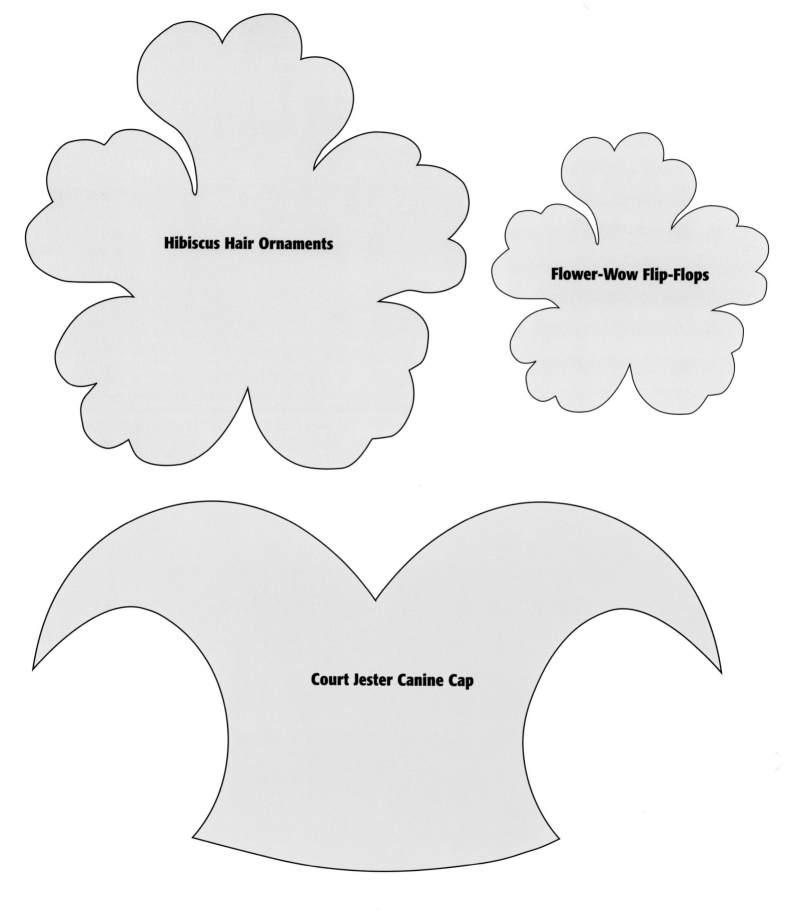

Hibiscus Hair Ornaments

Flower-Wow Flip-Flops

Court Jester Canine Cap

Index

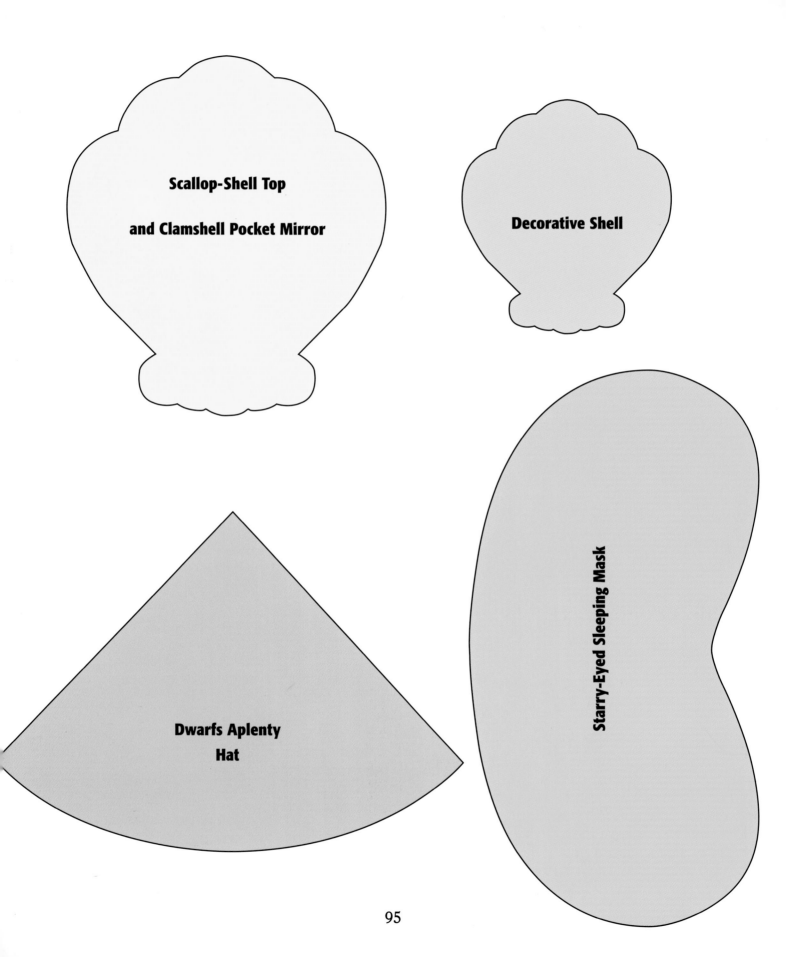

Scallop-Shell Top

and Clamshell Pocket Mirror

Decorative Shell

Dwarfs Aplenty
Hat

Starry-Eyed Sleeping Mask

95